Presented to

Beni Mendel

לרגל חגיגת סיומו

מסכת בבא קמא פרק כיצד הרגל

משניות מסכתות מגילה ויומא

פרשת חקת ובלק

ספר שמואל ב'

הלכות תפילין וימים טובים

יראת שמים and תורה May you grow in
for many years to come

רב מרדכי קמנצקי, ראש ישיבה
רב חנינא הרצברג, מנהל הישיבה
רב זאב דוידאויץ, מנהל המחינה
ר' גדעון למברגר, רבי

June 12, 2018 ♦ כט' סיון תשע"ח

THE CONCISE CHAFETZ CHAIM
a page a day

THE CONCISE CHAFETZ CHAIM

a page a day

FELDHEIM
JERUSALEM · NEW YORK

*A clear and concise presentation
of the laws of forbidden speech,
following the original format
of the Sefer Chafetz Chaim,
and divided into the daily learning schedule
of HaRav Yehudah Zev Segal zt"l,
the Manchester Rosh Yeshiva.*

With:
Pearls of Life
*Inspiring thoughts from our Sages
about the importance of guarding our speech.*

By Rabbi Asher Wasserman

*Author of the Derech Berurah
commentary on Mishnah Berurah;
Mishnas Avos commentary on Pirkei Avos;
and Concise Sefer HaChinuch*

Translated into English by Rabbi Daniel Worenklein
Halachic review by Rabbi Yisroel Krausz
Edited by Judy Lee
Page layout by Eden Chachamtzedek

ISBN 978-1-59826-187-5

Copyright © 2008 by Rabbi Asher Wasserman
Tel: 972-3-5793051
5 Noam Elimelech, Bnei Brak

All rights reserved.
No part of this publication may be translated,
reproduced, stored in a retrieval system or transmitted,
in any form or by any means, electronic, mechanical,
photocopying, recording, or otherwise, without
permission in writing from the author.

Distributed by:
FELDHEIM PUBLISHERS
POB 43163 / Jerusalem, Israel

208 Airport Executive Park
Nanuet, NY 10954

www.feldheim.com

Printed in Israel

מפרסמים עושי מצוה

הנגיד המפואר צנוע ומעלי
ראש וראשון לכל דבר שבקדושה
שייף עייל ושייף נפיק ולא מחזיק טיבותא לנפשיה

הר"ר **שמואל צבי יעקב באש** שליט"א
ורעייתו מרת **מרים** תחי'

אשר נטלו על עצמם הוצאת הספר
בשמחה ובנפש חפצה

לעילוי נשמת האבא
אוהב תורה ומוקיר רבנן
הר"ר **יהושע פאליק** ז"ל
בן
הר"ר **שמואל צבי** ז"ל
נלב"ע י"ז שבט תשמ"ב
ת.נ.צ.ב.ה.

יה"ר שזכות הרבים בחיזוק שמירת הלשון המקרבת את הגאולה
תעמוד לו ולרעייתו ולכל בני ביתו
לזכות לראות בנחמת ציון ובנין בית מקדשנו במהרה בימינו
מתוך בריאות הגוף והרחבת הדעת
פרנסה בשפע ונחת מכל יוצאי חלציהם
ואך טוב וחסד ירדפום כל ימי חייהם

כבוד חכמים ינחלו

We would like to express our sincere
thanks and appreciation to

The Admor of Brizdovitz *shlita*

who leads our community with
a strong and loving hand,
and whose shul is filled with the sounds
of Torah from morning until night.

May Hashem grant him good health
and long life, to continue his endeavors
of Torah, *tefillah* and *chesed*,
as is his heart's desire.

התודה והברכה

To our dear friends and patrons of
the *Derech Berurah* series:

Rav Baruch Yehudah Gross shlita
and his wife,
Rechel shetichyeh

In this merit, may they know only joy
and happiness in their home.
May they be blessed with success,
health and abundant *nachas*
from all their children.

Sponsors of the "Klalei Lashon Hara" Section
(as of this printing)

Foreword and Introduction:
In memory of
Rav Avraham Betzalel ben Rav Asher Zelig *z"l*
8 Tishrei, 5766

Prohibitions and Positive Commandments:
In memory of
Rav Yosef ben Rav Dov Zelikowitz *z"l*
1 Cheshvan, 5763

Klal 1:
In memory of
Mrs. Leah Feiga *bas* **R' Yaakov Hecht** *a"h*
8 Sivan, 5762

Klal 2:
In memory of
Mrs. Etel *bas* **Boruch** *a"h*
3rd day of Chanukah 5762

Klal 3:

Klal 4:

Klal 5:

Klal 6:

Klal 7:

Klal 8:

Klal 9:

Klal 10:

Sponsorship opportunities are available for future printings of this sefer.
Please call 718-663-1311 or 718-633-0433

Sponsors of the "Klalei Rechilus" Section
(as of this printing)

Klal 1:
In memory of
Rav Asher Zelig ben Rav Meir Dov z"l and Mrs. Henya Liba bas Rav Eliezer a"h
who were martyred in the Holocaust in sanctification of Hashem's Name

Klal 2:
In memory of
Rav Yisrael ben Rav Pinchas z"l
7 Cheshvan, 5718

Klal 3:
In memory of
Mrs. Buna bas Rav Rafael Gershon Tzvi a"h
17 Cheshvan, 5711
and her son, Yosef Dov
who were martyred in the Holocaust in sanctification of Hashem's Name

Klal 4:
In memory of
Rav Dov ben Rav Chaim
20 Tishrei, 5717

Klal 5:
In memory of
Mrs. Devorah bas Rav Gedaliah a"h
2 Adar I, 5703

Klal 6:
In memory of
Rav Yaakov ben Rav Moshe z"l, Mrs. Chentza bas Rav Yitzchak Eber z"l, and their son, Yitzchak Eber z"l
who were martyred in the Holocaust in sanctification of Hashem's Name

Klal 7:

Klal 8:

Klal 9:

Examples of Rechilus (Section):

Sponsorship opportunities are available for future printings of this sefer.
Please call 718-663-1311 or 718-633-0433

Blessing from Hagaon Hagadol

R. Yosef Shalom Elyashiv *shlita*

בס״ד, ג׳ אלול התשנ״ז

הרה״ג ר״א וסרמן שליט״א, הביא לפני רבינו מרן הגרי״ש אלישיב שליט״א פרי יגיעו בתורה, והוא חיבורו דרך ברורה, ובו מובאים הלכות וסיכומים מדברי המ״ב על כל סעיף וסעיף.

כבר העידו על נחיצות הספר הגאונים הרבנים שליט״א כפי המובא בהסכמותיהם, כי יהא הדבר לתועלת לרבים מלומדי המ״ב, וצירף מרן שליט״א ברכתו כי יזכה המחבר להתחיל ספרים אחרים ולסיימם לתועלת לומדי תוה״ק, מתוך נחת והרחבת הדעת.

לברכת התורה

יוסף ש. אלישיב

R. Elyashiv's letter of blessing was given to the author for a previous work.

The author presented the Hebrew manuscript of this sefer to Hagaon

R. Chaim Kanievsky *shlita*

who suggested the title: *Kitzur Chafetz Chaim.*

Rav Kanievsky said that the Chafetz Chaim made for us a *Shulchan Aruch* for the laws of *lashon hara,* and it is a great mitzvah to know these laws. He added that this concise version will be greatly beneficial to knowing and practicing these laws.

Translation of Approbation from Hagaon Hagadol
R. Chaim Pinchas Scheinberg *shlita*

BS"D   Teves, 5768

Rav Asher Wasserman has presented me with his writings on the laws of *lashon hara* and a selection of inspiring thoughts on the matter, based on the works of the great Torah leader, the Chafetz Chaim *zt"l*, translated into English, and divided into a daily learning schedule of two laws each day. His inspiring words have been written in a clear and pleasant language, appropriate for people of all backgrounds.

The author *shlita* has merited to enable Jews from all countries to establish a fixed practice of studying these crucial halachos each day. This study is the potion of life, as the *pasuk* states, "Who is the man that desires life?" (*Tehillim* 34). All those who make a fixed daily study of these laws will merit the continuation of the *pasuk*: "He loves days and sees good." By making a daily practice of learning these laws, the merit of the Torah study involved in these *halachos* will protect us from the terrible sin of *lashon hara*. "One who guards his mouth and tongue, guards his soul from suffering" (*Mishlei* 21:23). Certainly, anyone who desires true life will bring this blessing into his home, with gratitude to the author *shlita*, for the good he has done us.

I have only to bless the author that the wellsprings of his teachings may flow forth, and that he may merit to grace the public with many more similar writings, amidst good health and success.

For the honor of the Torah and its students,
Chaim Pinchas Scheinberg

Rabbi CHAIM P. SCHEINBERG	הרב חיים פינחס שייג ברג
Rosh Hayeshiva "TORAH ORE"	ראש ישיבת "תורה אור"
and Morah Hora'ah of Kiryat Mattersdorf	ומורה הוראה דקרית מטרסדורף

בס"ד

טבת תשס"ח

בא לפני האברך כמדרשו הרה"ג אשר וסרמן שליט"א ותכריך כתביו בידו סידור ועריכת "הלכות לשון הרע" ו"מאמרי שמירת הלשון" למרן רשכבה"ג החפץ חיים זצוק"ל בשפת האנגלית ע"פ סדר "דף ליום" הכולל "שני הלכות" ליום. ובצידו "מאמר החיזוק", הכל בשפה ברורה ונעימה דבר השוה לכל נפש.

וזכה המחבר שליט"א לזכות את הרבים בכל אתר ואתר באפשרות לקיים קביעות יומי בהלכות נחוצות אלו שהוא סמא דחיי, וכלשון הפסוק (תהלים לד) "מי האיש החפץ חיים" וגו'. ויזכו כל הקובעים עצמם בזה יום יום להמשך הפסוק (שם) "אוהב ימים לראות טוב" שע"י הלימוד היומי באופן תדיר זכות המצוה של ת"ת בענין זה מגני מפני חטאו החמור של לשון הרע. ו"כל השומר פיו ולשונו שומר מצרות נפשו" (משלי כא, כג). ובודאי שכל החפצים בחיים אמיתיים יזכו להביא ברכה זו אל ביתם ויודו להרב המחבר שליט"א על הטוב אשר שם לפניהם.

ואין לי אלא לברך שיופצו מעינותיך חוצה לזכות את הרבים בעוד חיבורים מועילים כהנה וכהנה מתוך בריאות גופא ונהורא מעליא וכ"ט סלה

הכו"ח לכבוד התורה ולומדי'ה

הרב חיים פנחס שייינברג
ראש ישיבת "תורה אור"
ומורה הוראה דקרית מטרסדורף
ירושלים

Approbation from Hagaon Hagadol
R. Nissim Karelitz shlita

הרב ש.י. נסים קרליץ
רמת - אהרון
רח' ר' מאיר 6 בני ברק

בס"ד, יום כ' שבט תשנ"ז

ראיתי את הספר שחיבר הרה"ג מוה"ר אשר וסרמן שליט"א שבו הביא הלכות השו"ע והמשנה ברורה באופן מסודר וברור כל הלכה והלכה בציון מקורה, **וזה דבר שלרבים יהיה תועלת מזה.** וכאשר חיבר הדבר ביגיעה רבה בדיבוק חברים ושימוש חכמים לברר כל פרט, **ראויים הדברים להדפיסם ולהפיצם בישראל.** ויהי רצון שיזכה הרב המחבר לגמור את אשר החל על כל אורח חיים ושאר חלקי התורה וזכות הרבים תהי' תלוי בו.

' remaining approbations were given to the author for previous works.

Approbations from Hagaon Hagadol
R. Shmuel haLevi Wosner *shlita*
and Hagaon R. Moshe Shaul Klein *shlita*

משה שאול קלייןּ
מו"ץ בבד"ץ דמרן הגר"ש ואזנר שליט"א
ורב שכונת אור-החיים בני-ברק

בס"ד יום י"ב בשבט תשנ"ז לפ"ק

הנה הרה"ג המופלג מאד מוה"ר אשר וסרמן שליט"א מתושבי שכונת "אור החיים" הגה בלבו **דבר טוב** לעשות סדר למשנה דהיינו לספר המשנה ברורה לעשות סיכומי דינים והלכות על כל סעיף וסעיף.

ויגע בזה טובא כדי להוציא משנה ברורה והלכה ברורה במקום אחד **ותועלת גדולה יש בזה ללומדי ההלכה** אחר שגמרו הסעיף במחבר ורמ"א ומ"ב ובה"ל ושעה"צ יהיה מסודר לפניהם כשולחן הערוך דינים היוצאים מהסעיף הנ"ל. ע"כ **יפה הוא עושה להעלות פרי יגיעתו עלי ספר לתועלת הלומדים**. ויה"ר שנזכה בזכות הרבצת תורה ובירור הלכה למה שכתוב: ומלאה הארץ דעה כמים לים מכסים.

וע"ז באתי על החתום לכבוד עמלי תורה

ב"ה
הרני מצטרף לדברים האמורים
למעלה בשבח המחבר שהוא מן
המיגעים מאד בתורה ונוצר תאנה
יאכל פרי'
ע"ז בעה"ח מצפה לישועה
שמואל הלוי ואזנר

Approbation from Hagaon Hagadol
R. Moshe Halberstam ztz"l

משה הלברשטאם

חבר בית דין צדק העדה החרדית
ראש ישיבת "דברי חיים" טשאקאווע
מח"ס שו"ת "דברי משה"
פעיה"ק ירושלים תובב"א
רח' יואל 8 טל. 5370514

הן בא לפני הרה"ג חוב"ט ולן בעומקה של הלכה כש"ת הרב אשר וסרמן שליט"א מטובי הלומדים בעיה"ת בני ברק, ובידו תכריך כתבים מלא דבר ה' זו הלכה לפי סדר המשנה ברורה, ואחר שכבוד ב"א חביבי ויקירי מאד נעלה הרה"ג רבי סיני הלברשטאם שליט"א מורה ודאין בב"י עיין בזה היטב, הביע לפני התפעלותו מגודל היגיעה והעיון שהשקיע המחבר הנ"ל בכדי להוציא מתח"י דבר שלם, **וראיתי בספר הזה את התועלת הגדולה להההוגים בספר משנה ברורה שיהא להם ערוך ומסודר עד להפליא ובודאי רבים וכן טובים יביאו את הברכה לתוך ביתם**, ושכרו כפול מן השמים, שיהי' תמיד מן המזכים את הרבים, ולהמשיך לשבת בבית ה' וללמוד וללמד ולהוציא לאור עולם מעיינותיו חוצה מתוך נחת והרחבה, אמן כיה"ר.

ובעה"ח לכבוד עמלה של תורה ודבר ה' זו הלכה, היום יום ג' שנכפבכ"ט לסדר אשר יעשה אותם האדם וחי בהם וגו',

אסרו חג דפסח, שנת ציון המצוינת לפי"ק.

Contents

Author's Preface 17
Foreword 23
Introduction to the Laws of Lashon Hara and Rechilus 30

❖ The Laws of Lashon Hara ❖

KLAL 1: The Prohibition of Speaking *Lashon Hara*, and the Severity of Its Punishment 48

KLAL 2: *Lashon Hara* Spoken in the Presence of Three People 52

KLAL 3: *Lashon Hara* in the Subject's Presence, as a Joke, or without Revealing the Subject's Name 59

KLAL 4: *Lashon Hara* regarding Faults in Religious Observance 63

KLAL 5: *Lashon Hara* regarding Faults in Matters *Bein Adam L'Chaveiro* 70

KLAL 6: Listening to and Believing *Lashon Hara* 75

KLAL 7: Details of the Laws of Accepting *Lashon Hara* 81

KLAL 8: The Subject and Audience of *Lashon Hara* 89

KLAL 9: *Avak Lashon Hara* 97

KLAL 10: *Lashon Hara* regarding Matters *Bein Adam L'Chaveiro* 101

❧ The Laws of Rechilus ❧

KLAL 1:	The Prohibition Against Speaking *Rechilus*	110
KLAL 2:	Public *Rechilus*	116
KLAL 3:	*Rechilus* in the Subject's Presence or Absence	118
KLAL 4:	*Rechilus* Known to the Subject	120
KLAL 5:	Listening to and Accepting *Rechilus*	121
KLAL 6:	Additional Rules of *Rechilus*	125
KLAL 7:	The Speaker and the Audience of *Rechilus*	129
KLAL 8:	*Avak Rechilus*	133
KLAL 9:	When *Rechilus* Is Permitted	135
	Lashon Hara in Business	143
	Lashon Hara regarding *Shidduchim*	145

Index 149

Author's Preface

WITH PRAISE AND THANKSGIVING to Hashem Yisbarach, we present before the public this English translation of *Kitzur Chafetz Chaim*.

The idea for this project developed as a result of our *Derech Berurah* commentary on *Chafetz Chaim*, which explains and summarizes the laws of *lashon hara*. These synopses were then woven into *Kitzur Chafetz Chaim*, an abridged version of *Chafetz Chaim*, tailor made for today's "on-the-go" generation. It contains the halachic rulings of the *Chafetz Chaim*, focusing on the points that are most relevant in our day-to-day conversations. The wording was designed to be as clear and concise as possible.

⚜ ⚜ ⚜

Kitzur Chafetz Chaim is divided into a daily learning schedule in which each day's session is contained on one page, and can be learned in just a minute or two. No one should find it too difficult to make time in his busy schedule to dedicate these few minutes to this important subject. The Chafetz Chaim himself writes that the success and safety of the Jewish people depends on adherance to these laws.

The *sefer* follows a four-month learning program, according to the Hebrew year, based on the schedule designed by Rav Yehudah Zev Segal *zt"l*, the Manchester Rosh Yeshiva. A calendar on the top of each page details what should be read daily, completing three cycles each year. The dates on the lower portion of the calendar apply to a leap year.

The *halachos* contained in this text correspond exactly to the *halachos* in the original *Chafetz Chaim,* thus allowing the reader to easily pursue further research in the original source.

Following the pattern of the original Chafetz Chaim, this *sefer* is divided into two sections: the laws of *lashon hara* and the laws of *rechilus*, each of which are further divided into *Klalim* (chapters).

Bold print headings for each new subject help the reader easily navigate through the text. Attached to each day's lesson is a "Pearl of Life," an inspiring thought from the Chafetz Chaim or from our Sages, to encourage us in our pursuit of pure speech.

❊   ❊   ❊

Kitzur Chafetz Chaim was composed in order to assist people of all backgrounds to set a fixed schedule each day to learn these important *halachos*. For those who find it difficult to learn the original *Chafetz Chaim*, or do not have the time to do so, this *sefer* will be of great value. Even for those who do learn the original *Chafetz Chaim*, the *Kitzur* version can help summarize the most essential points.

Many shuls have started the admirable practice of learning together a portion of *Chafetz Chaim* each day after davening, or between *Minchah* and *Maariv*. This sefer is ideal for finding prepared *shiurim* suitable for these learning sessions.

In the family, *Kitzur Chafetz Chaim* can be used as a bonding agent. Husband and wife can study it together over dinner, and learn it with their children. One woman told us that she calls her husband at work every day to study with him their "one-minute-*chavrusa*" in *Kitzur Chafetz Chaim*. In schools and work places, classes in *Kitzur Chafetz Chaim* have become commonplace.

The original Hebrew version of this *sefer* was first published in 5766, and was warmly received by the Hebrew-speaking public in Eretz Yisrael. We have since received countless responses from people of all backgrounds, Torah scholars and laymen alike — men, women and children. They found the *sefer* a clear and easy way to study the laws of *lashon hara*.

❊   ❊   ❊

Tremendous effort has been invested to publish this *sefer*, with the hopes that it will be found useful by the public. The translation was composed under the guidance of gifted Torah scholars, with an eye for both halachic accuracy and clarity of language. We call out to every Jew who cares about the welfare of Klal Yisrael, to set aside a fixed time each day to study the laws of *lashon hara*, either in the original *Chafetz Chaim* or in the *Kitzur Chafetz Chaim*. It is our sincere hope that this English translation, *The Concise Chafetz Chaim*, will also be well received and will be a practical benefit to all those who study it.

Our Sages tell us that even if a person restrains himself from forbidden speech for just a mere moment, he will merit the special hidden light reserved for those who guard their tongue — as we see from the words of Midrash, quoted by the Vilna Gaon: "For every single moment that a person guards his mouth from speaking forbidden words, he merits to enjoy a hidden light that no angel could possibly fathom."

May this *sefer* be of great benefit to promote the strengthening of guarding one's tongue. In this merit may Hashem bestow upon us all the blessings promised to those who successfully control their speech.

Asher Wasserman
Bnei Brak
Tu B'Shvat 5768

Prayer for Proper Speech

⸙ תְּפִלָּה עַל הַדִּבּוּר ⸙

רִבּוֹנוֹ שֶׁל עוֹלָם יְהִי רָצוֹן מִלְּפָנֶיךָ אֵל רַחוּם וְחַנּוּן, שֶׁתְּזַכֵּנִי הַיּוֹם וּבְכָל יוֹם לִשְׁמֹר פִּי וּלְשׁוֹנִי מִלָּשׁוֹן הָרָע וּרְכִילוּת.

וְאֶזָּהֵר מִלְּדַבֵּר אֲפִלּוּ עַל אִישׁ יְחִידִי, וְכָל שֶׁכֵּן עַל כְּלַל יִשְׂרָאֵל, אוֹ עַל חֵלֶק מֵהֶם. וְכָל שֶׁכֵּן מִלְּהִתְרָעֵם עַל מִדּוֹתָיו שֶׁל הַקָּדוֹשׁ בָּרוּךְ הוּא. וְאֶזָּהֵר מִלְּדַבֵּר דִּבְרֵי שֶׁקֶר, מַחֲלוֹקֶת, כַּעַס, גַּאֲוָה, אוֹנָאַת דְּבָרִים, הַלְבָּנַת פָּנִים, לֵצָנוּת, וְכָל דִּבּוּר אָסוּר.

וְזַכֵּנִי שֶׁלֹּא לְדַבֵּר כִּי אִם דָּבָר הַצָּרִיךְ לְעִנְיְנֵי גוּפִי וְנַפְשִׁי, וְיִהְיוּ כָּל מַעֲשַׂי וְדִבּוּרַי לְשֵׁם שָׁמַיִם.

⸙ ⸙ ⸙

(מהגה"צ רַבִּי שְׁמוּאֵל הוֹמִינֶר זצ"ל עַל פִּי הַנֻּסָּח שֶׁסִּדֵּר רַבֵּנוּ הֶחָפֵץ חַיִּים זצ"ל)

THE
CONCISE
CHAFETZ
CHAIM
a page a day

| Daily Calendar | I TISHREI | I SHVAT | I SIVAN |
| Leap Year | I TISHREI | II SHVAT | 20 IYAR |

Foreword

1. Blessed is Hashem, God of Israel, Who distinguished us from all nations, granted us the Torah, and brought us to Eretz Yisrael, so that we may perform all His mitzvos. Hashem's intention was solely for our benefit, to sanctify us unto Him and thereby grant us great blessing in this world and the next.

2. Not only did He grant us the Torah, He also commanded us never to forsake it. He appointed prophets to admonish us and help us improve our ways. Yet, at the end of the era of the second Beis HaMikdash, our nation was plagued with senseless hatred and *lashon hara*, which led to the destruction of the Beis HaMikdash and our exile from our land.

> ### ❧ *Pearls of Life* ❧
>
> If a person uses a limb of his body to perform a mitzvah in this world, Hashem's radiance will rest upon that limb in the World to Come. However, if he forsakes one of the two hundred and forty eight positive commandments (which correspond to the two hundred and forty eight limbs of the body), and does not do *teshuvah* (repent), then his soul will lack the corresponding spiritual "limb" in the World to Come.
>
> Therefore, if a person joins the ranks of those who speak *lashon hara*, and gives free rein to his mouth and ears to speak and hear *lashon hara*, he will be punished in the World to Come by having these faculties impaired.
>
> (*Shemiras HaLashon*, Introduction)

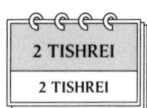 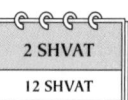 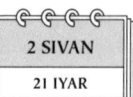

| 2 TISHREI | 2 SHVAT | 2 SIVAN | Daily Calendar |
| 2 TISHREI | 12 SHVAT | 21 IYAR | Leap Year |

3. From the time we were exiled from our land, we have been praying and longing each day that Hashem may at last redeem us, but our prayers have not yet been answered. There are many sins responsible for the length of the Exile, but the sin of *lashon hara* rises above them all. Since the Exile was caused by *lashon hara*, the Redemption cannot come until we correct it.

4. Hashem will not rest His blessings upon us while we defile ourselves by speaking *lashon hara*, after He has written an explicit curse in His Torah against those who speak *lashon hara* (in addition to the other curses often involved in *lashon hara*, as discussed below).

   Our Sages tell us that the damage wrought by *lashon hara* is inestimable. When a person contemplates the teachings of our Sages from the Gemara and Zohar, which discuss the terrible effects of *lashon hara*, he is horrified by its atrocity.

✣ *Pearls of Life* ✣

If, *chas v'shalom*, a person's speech or hearing became damaged, it would cause him more anguish than the loss of any organ, since these two faculties are so crucial. All the more so would a person suffer great anguish in the World to Come if his powers of speech or hearing were impaired there as a result of his sins. How much humiliation would he suffer! All would know the reason for his disabilities — that he spoke words of *lashon hara* and controversy during his time in this world.

(*Shemiras HaLashon*, Introduction)

Daily Calendar	3 TISHREI	3 SHVAT	3 SIVAN
Leap Year	3 TISHREI	13 SHVAT	22 IYAR

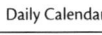
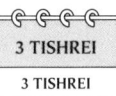
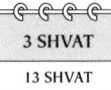
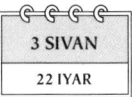

5. The Torah so strictly forbids *lashon hara* because it awakens the Satan to raise accusations against the Jewish people. These accusations can even lead to untimely death.

6. Another reason *lashon hara* is so destructive is that when a person sullies his mouth with forbidden speech, it prevents his holy words of Torah and prayer from ascending to Heaven.

   If many people constantly speak *lashon hara*, repeating this sin thousands of times over the course of their lives, and making no commitment to refrain from it, this wreaks inestimable damage upon the Higher Worlds.

❧ *Pearls of Life* ❧

If a person regularly repeats this sin, it will be very difficult for him to find a recourse to correct his deeds. Our Sages tell us that in the future, everyone will be healed except for those who regularly spoke *lashon hara*. Their souls will forever suffer terrible humiliation.

Rebbe Shimon bar Yochai taught that even Miriam was punished for speaking *lashon hara* against Moshe, although she did not intend to slander him, but spoke only for his own good. All the more so will the wicked be punished for speaking *lashon hara* to slander their fellows and ruin their lives.

(*Shemiras HaLashon*, Introduction)

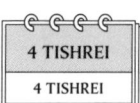 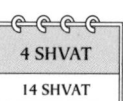 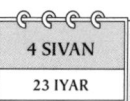

| 4 TISHREI | 4 SHVAT | 4 SIVAN | Daily Calendar |
| 4 TISHREI | 14 SHVAT | 23 IYAR | Leap Year |

7. The prohibition against *lashon hara* is neglected by many people, due to two different ploys of the *yetzer hara*:

   a. It tells us that the comment in question is not considered *lashon hara*.

   b. Alternatively, it tells us that the Torah permits speaking *lashon hara* against the person in question.

8. Sometimes the *yetzer hara* employs the opposite tactic. It makes the laws of *lashon hara* seem excessively strict. A person is then led to believe that everything is considered *lashon hara*, and he cannot lead a normal life if he wishes to observe these laws.

9. Furthermore, many people lack basic knowledge of the laws against accepting *lashon hara*. For example, many do not know that it is forbidden to believe *lashon hara*, even if one makes no visible sign of consent.

   For all these reasons, the entire subject of refraining from *lashon hara* has fallen to the wayside. People have become accustomed to freely speak as they wish, without first considering if their words constitute *lashon hara* or *rechilus*. We have become so accustomed to *lashon hara* that many people do not even consider it a sin at all.

❧ *Pearls of Life* ❧

Through Torah study, the damage caused by *lashon hara* can be repaired to some extent. The Gemara states (*Arachin* 15b): "How can speakers of *lashon hara* correct their deeds? If they are Torah scholars, let them toil in Torah, as the verse says, 'A healing for the tongue is the Tree of Life' (*Mishlei* 15:4)."

(*Shemiras HaLashon, Shaar HaTorah*, ch. 1)

Daily Calendar	5 TISHREI	5 SHVAT	5 SIVAN
Leap Year	5 TISHREI	15 SHVAT	24 IYAR

10. This *sefer* is divided into two sections: (a) the laws of *lashon hara* and (b) the laws of *rechilus*. Although the laws of *rechilus* may generally be inferred from the laws of *lashon hara*, it is necessary to reiterate them in the second section because of the great prevalence of *lashon hara* and the need for clear guidelines regarding what is permitted and what is forbidden.

11. The Chafetz Chaim authored a companion volume entitled *Shemiras HaLashon*. There, he compiled the teachings of our Sages regarding *lashon hara*, including the great reward for refraining from *lashon hara*, and the terrible punishment for speaking or accepting it.

> ### ⁂ *Pearls of Life* ⁂
>
> It is not enough simply to learn *mussar* in order to help us refrain from *lashon hara*. We must also learn the laws of what is considered *lashon hara*. What good is all the *mussar* in the world, which warns of the terrible prohibition of *lashon hara* and *rechilus*, if a person permits himself with baseless excuses that "This is not considered *lashon hara*," or "The Torah permits *lashon hara* about that person"?
>
> (*Shemiras HaLashon*, Introduction)

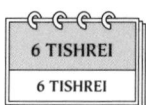 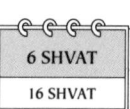 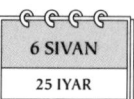

| 6 TISHREI | 6 SHVAT | 6 SIVAN | Daily Calendar |
| 6 TISHREI | 16 SHVAT | 25 IYAR | Leap Year |

12. There is a well-known Midrash that if a person toils in studying the words of our Sages, Hashem protects him from the *yetzer hara*. Perhaps by studying this book, in which the laws of *lashon hara* are compiled, the *yetzer hara* will have less sway in enticing us to speak or accept *lashon hara*. By distancing ourselves from *lashon hara* even slightly, over the course of time we will come to shun *lashon hara* entirely, since habit has much influence in this area. When a person seeks to purify himself of sin, Hashem assists him.

❧ *Pearls of Life* ❧

The *yetzer hara* discourages us from learning and practicing *shemiras halashon*. "What benefit will you have from studying these matters?" it asks. "Will you ever be able to observe these laws properly and refrain from speaking *lashon hara* for the rest of your life? It is doubtful whether you will be able to refrain for even a day or two. Better not to begin at all."

To dispute these claims, our Sages tell us, "Do not distance yourself from a good trait, even if you will not be able to master it" (*Avos d'Rabbi Nasan*).

(*Shemiras HaLashon*, Introduction)

On the second and third cycle of the year, the following page should also be learned.

| Daily Calendar | 7 TISHREI | 6 SHVAT | 6 SIVAN |
| Leap Year | 7 TISHREI | 16 SHVAT | 25 IYAR |

On the second and third cycle of the year,
this page is learned in addition to the previous one.

13. Some may dismiss the importance of learning these laws by citing the saying of our Sages: "Better to transgress unintentionally than to be informed of the law and transgress it nonetheless." However, this saying does not apply to mitzvos that are explicit in the Torah (see *Shulchan Aruch*, O.C. 608:2), such as the prohibition against *lashon hara* and *rechilus*. Furthermore, according to this warped reasoning, we should also not learn the laws of Shabbos and theft, since these too are difficult to observe.

14. The Torah understands the depths of our nature and reveals to us that we are indeed capable of guarding our tongues. Hashem would not obligate us in a mitzvah that we are incapable of observing. If He commanded us to refrain from *lashon hara* and *rechilus*, surely we can.

15. Another benefit of learning these laws is that *shemiras halashon* will at least not be forsaken entirely. Even if a person does speak *lashon hara* on occasion, he will not be considered a *baal lashon hara* — a habitual speaker of *lashon hara*. When our Sages tell us that *lashon hara* is equivalent to idolatry, illicit relations, and murder, and that a person who speaks *lashon hara* will not merit to behold the *Shechinah* (among the many other terrible results of *lashon hara*), they refer to those who habitually speak *lashon hara*.

In the merit of learning and observing the laws
of lashon hara, may the Redeemer come to Tzion,
speedily in our days. Amen.

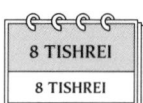 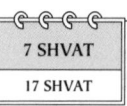 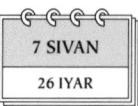

| 8 TISHREI | 7 SHVAT | 7 SIVAN | Daily Calendar |
| 8 TISHREI | 17 SHVAT | 26 IYAR | Leap Year |

Introduction to the Laws of Lashon Hara and Rechilus

1. In Hashem's great love for His nation, Israel, and in His fervent desire for our benefit, He distanced us from all harmful traits, especially *lashon hara* and *rechilus*. These traits promote strife and dispute, which may even lead to bloodshed. Many terrible evils result from these despicable traits.

2. The current Exile is due primarily to the sin of the spies who were sent to investigate Eretz Yisrael. Our Sages tell us that the spies sinned by speaking *lashon hara* against the Land. Furthermore, during the days of Rebbe Shimon ben Shetach, *rechilus* led to a terrible calamity in which the Sages of Israel were slaughtered. The city of Beitar was also destroyed by *lashon hara* and *rechilus*. Countless other terrible tragedies have been caused by *lashon hara*.

> ### ❧ Pearls of Life ❧
>
> It has been tried and proven that if a person applies himself to *shemiras halashon*, the more he grows accustomed to it, the easier it becomes. He will begin to notice the improper words that leave his mouth, whereas he had previously taken no notice, due to his habit of speaking as he pleased. After breaking the habit of *lashon hara*, with just a slight effort, he can refrain from speaking forbidden words.
>
> (*Shemiras HaLashon*, Introduction)

Daily Calendar	9 TISHREI	8 SHVAT	8 SIVAN
Leap Year	9 TISHREI	18 SHVAT	27 IYAR

3. Due to the many terrible results of this trait, the Torah explicitly forbids it, as the verse states: "Do not go as a talebearer amongst your nation" (*Vayikra* 19:16).

Furthermore, *lashon hara* and *rechilus* can lead one to transgress almost all the commandments *bein adam l'chaveiro* (between man and his fellow) and many commandments *bein adam l'Makom* (between man and God). For this reason the Torah warns us not to fall into the dangerous snare of *lashon hara*.

Perhaps by clearly setting forth the many prohibitions and positive commandments involved in *lashon hara*, we will realize the severe consequences of our speech and thereby defeat the *yetzer hara*.

꙳ *Pearls of Life* ꙳

Throughout one's life, one must wage battle against his *yetzer hara*. This was the intention of our Sages when they said: "Let a person always incite his *yetzer tov* against his *yetzer hara*." This is also the intention of the verse "If the spirit of the tyrant rises against you, do not abandon your place" (*Koheles* 10:4).

(*Shemiras HaLashon*, Introduction)

❖ ❖ ❖

It is better to be thrown into a fiery furnace, than to publicly embarrass another person.

(*Berachos* 43b)

Introduction to the Laws

 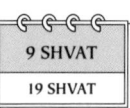 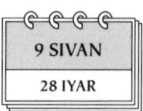

| Daily Calendar |
| Leap Year |

THE SEVENTEEN PROHIBITIONS OF *LASHON HARA*

1. **"Do not go as a talebearer amongst your nation"** (*Vayikra* 19:16).

   If a person goes from one friend to another bearing tales such as "This is what he said about you," or "This is what he did to you" (which is called *rechilus*); or if he speaks derogatorily of someone (which is called *lashon hara*), regardless of whether the subject of his remark is present — he transgresses the Torah prohibition, "Do not go as a talebearer amongst your nation."

2. **"Do not bear false testimony"** (*Shemos* 23:1).

   If a person speaks or accepts *lashon hara* or *rechilus*, he transgresses the Torah prohibition, "Do not bear false testimony." This prohibition is transgressed whether the information is true or false and whether or not the subject of the remark is present.

❖ *Pearls of Life* ❖

Anyone with common sense will endeavor to constantly wage war against his *yetzer hara* in order not to fall into the snare of the terrible sin of *lashon hara*. Fortunate will be his portion in this world and the next.

(*Shemiras HaLashon, Zechirah*, ch. 4)

3. **"Guard yourself from the plague of *tzara'as* by being exceedingly careful and diligent"** (*Devarim* 24:8).

   As was the case with Miriam, *lashon hara* is punished by *tzara'as* (a hideous skin condition that causes ritual impurity). The Torah warns us against *lashon hara* in order that we be spared this plague.

4. **"Do not place a stumbling block before the blind"** (*Vayikra* 19:14).

   a. The Torah commands us not to physically or spiritually harm an unwitting victim. By speaking *lashon hara* or *rechilus*, one places a stumbling block before others by causing them to transgress the prohibition of listening to *lashon hara*. The more people who hear the *lashon hara*, the greater is his sin.

   b. A person who listens to *lashon hara* may also be guilty of "placing a stumbling block before the blind." He encourages the speaker to sin by providing an audience for his *lashon hara*. If he is the only person listening, this is certainly true. If others are also listening, perhaps he is not responsible for the speaker's sin (since even without him, the speaker would have had an audience). However, the first person present to hear the *lashon hara* does violate this prohibition, even if other listeners arrive after him.

   c. In any case, one must be extremely careful not to sit in the company of those who speak *lashon hara*, since they are all inscribed together in Heaven as a "society of evil-doers."

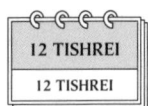 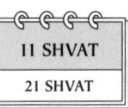 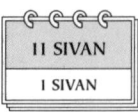

| 12 TISHREI | 11 SHVAT | 11 SIVAN | Daily Calendar |
| 12 TISHREI | 21 SHVAT | 1 SIVAN | Leap Year |

5. **"Guard yourself, lest you forget Hashem, your God"** (*Devarim* 8:11).

Our Sages interpret this verse as a remonstration against arrogance (*Sotah* 4b). A person can become haughty only if he forgets his insignificance relative to the infinite greatness of Hashem. *Lashon hara* often stems from a person's inflated sense of superiority, especially if he seeks honor by humiliating others. By doing so, one forfeits his portion in the World to Come (*Talmud Yerushalmi, Chagigah* 2:1).

6. **"Do not desecrate My holy Name"** (*Vayikra* 22:32).

For other sins, one could attempt to excuse himself by claiming that he fell prey to his own base desires. Yet this excuse does not apply to *lashon hara*, from which one derives no physical benefit. As such, speaking or accepting *lashon hara* shows one's utter disregard for Hashem's will. This creates a terrible *chilul Hashem*, especially when *lashon hara* is spoken or accepted by a respected person. When a person speaks or accepts *lashon hara* in public, it is considered a public desecration of Hashem's Name.

❧ *Pearls of Life* ❧

Just as the reward for Torah study is equal to the reward for all other mitzvos, the punishment for *lashon hara* is equal to the punishment for all other sins.

(*Talmud Yerushalmi*, cited in *Shemiras HaLashon*, Zechirah, ch. 1)

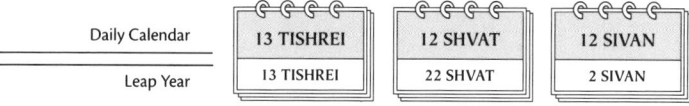

Daily Calendar	13 TISHREI	12 SHVAT	12 SIVAN
Leap Year	13 TISHREI	22 SHVAT	2 SIVAN

7. **"Do not hate your brother in your heart"** (*Vayikra* 19:17).

If a person pretends to be another's friend and then speaks against him behind his back, he transgresses the prohibition against secretly harboring hatred. This is especially true if he warns his audience not to tell the subject.

8–9. **"Do not take vengeance, and do not bear a grudge"** (*Vayikra* 19:18).

   a. **The speaker:** If a person speaks *lashon hara* out of resentment toward the subject for having failed to do him a favor, he transgresses this prohibition.

   b. **The listener:** If the listener encourages or enjoys hearing *lashon hara* due to resentment he feels toward the subject for failing to do him a favor, he transgresses this prohibition.

❦ *Pearls of Life* ❦

The *Tikkunei Zohar* states that *lashon hara* can reduce one to poverty, *chas v'shalom*. Therefore, if a person wishes to live comfortably, he should guard himself from speaking or accepting *lashon hara*.

(*Shemiras HaLashon, Zechirah*, ch. 6)

❖ ❖ ❖

The Holy One Blessed Be He desires no dealings with a *baal lashon hara* and does not wish to save him from misfortune. Therefore, a person has no choice but to guard his tongue from speaking evil.

(*Shemiras HaLashon, Zechirah*, ch. 4, citing the Midrash)

Introduction to the Laws

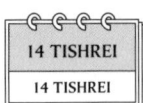 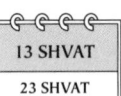 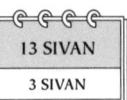

| 14 TISHREI | 13 SHVAT | 13 SIVAN | Daily Calendar |
| 14 TISHREI | 23 SHVAT | 3 SIVAN | Leap Year |

10. **"A single witness may not stand against a man for any sin or any transgression"** (*Devarim* 19:15).

    According to Torah law, testimony is acceptable in Beis Din only if it is offered by two or more witnesses. Since the testimony of a single witness is of no practical significance, it is considered mere slander. A single witness who offers testimony in Beis Din transgresses this prohibition.

11. **"Do not follow the multitude to sin"** (*Shemos* 23:2).

    If a person associates himself with gossipers in order to speak or hear *lashon hara*, he violates this prohibition. He also transgresses the positive commandment to associate with Torah scholars (as discussed below, in positive commandment 6).

✣ *Pearls of Life* ✣

If the *yetzer hara* succeeds in making you speak *lashon hara* today, then endeavor to overcome it tomorrow. If, *chas v'shalom*, it succeeds again tomorrow, then strengthen yourself to overcome it the next day.

(*Shemiras HaLashon*, Introduction)

✣ ✣ ✣

For every single moment that a person guards his mouth [from speaking forbidden words], he merits to enjoy a hidden light that no angel could possibly fathom.

(*Iggeres HaGra*, citing a Midrash)

| Daily Calendar | 15 TISHREI | 14 SHVAT | 14 SIVAN |
| Leap Year | 15 TISHREI | 24 SHVAT | 4 SIVAN |

12. **"Do not be like Korach and his followers"** (*Bemidbar* 17:5).

   If a person provokes controversy by speaking *lashon hara*, he transgresses this prohibition. (The person who accepts *lashon hara* might also transgress this prohibition).

13. **"Do not your distress your kinsman"** (*Vayikra* 25:17).

   If a person embarrasses someone by speaking about his past deeds, his family, his lack of intelligence, or any other upsetting flaws, he transgresses this prohibition. The same applies to *rechilus*; if a person tells someone how another spoke against him, he transgresses this prohibition. It is forbidden to do so in private, and it is even worse to do so in public.

❧ *Pearls of Life* ❧

Our Sages tell us that the second Beis HaMikdash was destroyed as a result of senseless hatred and *lashon hara*. If these sins could destroy the Beis HaMikdash, they can certainly prevent it from being rebuilt.

(*Shemiras HaLashon*, ch. 4)

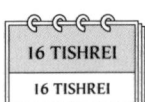  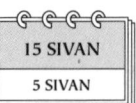

| 16 TISHREI | 15 SHVAT | 15 SIVAN | Daily Calendar |
| 16 TISHREI | 25 SHVAT | 5 SIVAN | Leap Year |

14. **"Do not bear a sin because of him"** (*Vayikra* 19:17).

    This verse teaches us that even when rebuking another for his sins, we must not embarrass him. If a person embarrasses another and causes him to blush, he violates this prohibition. If he does so in public, he forfeits his portion in the World to Come.

15. **"Do not afflict a widow or orphan"** (*Shemos* 22:21).

    a. If a person speaks even truthful *lashon hara* or *rechilus* against a widow or orphan in his presence, thereby hurting his feelings, he transgresses this prohibition. His punishment is explicit in the Torah, "My anger will flare, and I will kill you" (*Shemos* 22:23). (Rashi seems to imply that this prohibition applies not only to widows and orphans but also to any unfortunate person.)

    b. If widows or orphans are insulted to their face and one does not object, he will also be punished.

❧ *Pearls of Life* ❧

Hashem is more exacting with the sin of *lashon hara* than with any other sin. As Rebbe Shimon bar Yochai taught in the Zohar: "Hashem is prepared to forgive anything except *lashon hara.*"

(*Shemiras HaLashon, Zechirah*, ch. 2)

16. **"Do not bring guilt (תחניפו) upon the land"** (*Bemidbar* 35:33).

   a. The word תחניפו also means "flatter." The Rishonim learn from here that it is forbidden by Torah law to flatter the wicked. If a person speaks *lashon hara* or *rechilus* in order to impress someone who hates the subject, he violates this prohibition.

   b. When a person hears *lashon hara* and nods in agreement or adds words of encouragement to impress the speaker, he also transgresses this prohibition. Upon hearing *lashon hara*, one must be extremely careful not to make any sign of consent. If his rebuke might be accepted, he must rebuke the speaker for telling *lashon hara*.

17. **"Do not curse the deaf"** (*Vayikra* 19:14).

   When angrily speaking *lashon hara*, it is very common to curse the subject using Hashem's Name. If one does so, he violates this prohibition, even if he uses Hashem's Name in a foreign language. This prohibition applies whether or not the subject is deaf and whether or not he is present.

SUMMARY

We have listed here seventeen prohibitions that can be violated by speaking lashon hara. Some are punishable with death by the Heavenly Court. For others, one loses his portion in the World to Come. It is important to note that if one tells a gentile lashon hara about a Jew, his sin is far worse.

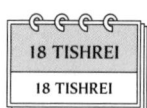 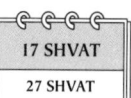 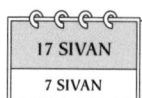

18 TISHREI / 18 TISHREI	Daily Calendar
17 SHVAT / 27 SHVAT	
17 SIVAN / 7 SIVAN	Leap Year

THE FOURTEEN POSITIVE COMMANDMENTS INVOLVED IN *LASHON HARA*

1. **"Remember what Hashem, your God, did to Miriam"** (*Devarim* 24:9).

   The Torah commands us to verbally recall the punishment Miriam received for speaking *lashon hara*. This is to remind us to distance ourselves from this severe sin. A person who speaks *lashon hara* or *rechilus* violates this positive commandment.

2. **"Love your neighbor as yourself"** (*Vayikra* 19:18).

   The Torah commands us to love every single Jew from the depths of our hearts and to guard his honor. One must speak only complimentary words of others, just as he would want them to speak of him. If a person speaks or accepts *lashon hara* or *rechilus* about another Jew, he clearly shows that he does not love that person as himself, and therefore he violates this mitzvah.

❖ *Pearls of Life* ❖

A person who speaks against someone greater than himself invites harm and even *tzara'as*. A proof for this can be learned from Miriam, who spoke against Moshe and was punished with *tzara'as*. Her punishment serves as a warning to all who engage in *lashon hara*.

(*Shemiras HaLashon, Zechirah*, ch. 5)

Daily Calendar	19 TISHREI	18 SHVAT	18 SIVAN
Leap Year	19 TISHREI	28 SHVAT	8 SIVAN

3. **"With righteousness, you shall judge your fellow"** (*Vayikra* 19:15).

   The Torah requires us to judge others favorably. If someone is known to be of average moral character, and the case against him seems equally balanced between guilt and innocence, we are required to judge him favorably. If he is known to be a God-fearing Jew, then we must judge him favorably, even if the situation seems weighted against him. A person who jumps to unwarranted conclusions and speaks *lashon hara* against another (or accepts another's unwarranted conclusions), when he should have judged favorably, violates this mitzvah.

4. **"Support him that he may dwell and live beside you.... Let your brother live with you"** (*Vayikra* 25:35–36).

   We are commanded to support others, to ensure that they do not lose their livelihood. If a person speaks *lashon hara* by saying that someone is unskilled or dishonest, thereby costing him his livelihood, he violates this mitzvah.

❧ *Pearls of Life* ❧

If one wishes to judge another favorably, he will always be able to find a way to justify questionable behavior.

(*Be'er Mayim Chaim*, positive commandment 3; there, the Chafetz Chaim cites numerous suggestions as to how to judge others favorably)

❧ ❧ ❧

The Torah assessed the depths of man's powers and realized that he is indeed capable of refraining from this sin.

(*Chafetz Chaim*, Introduction)

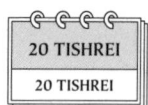 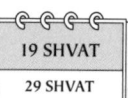 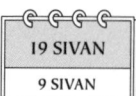

| 20 TISHREI | 19 SHVAT | 19 SIVAN | Daily Calendar |
| 20 TISHREI | 29 SHVAT | 9 SIVAN | Leap Year |

5. **"Rebuke your fellow"** (*Vayikra* **19:17**).

   If a person hears someone speaking *lashon hara* or *rechilus*, he must rebuke him to prevent him from sinning (if there is any chance that his attempt will be successful). One may not wait until the other person has finished speaking *lashon hara* and then rebuke him. He must interrupt immediately.

6. **"Cling to Him"** (*Devarim* **10:20**).

   The Torah commands us to cling to Hashem, by associating with Torah scholars. If a person instead associates with people who discuss *lashon hara*, he violates this mitzvah.

❧ *Pearls of Life* ❧

Just as each *k'zayis* (olive-size piece) of pork is a sin unto itself, so too is each word of slander.

(*Chafetz Chaim*, positive commandment 3)

❧   ❧   ❧

Do not disdain any person.

(*Avos* 4:3)

Daily Calendar	21 TISHREI	20 SHVAT	20 SIVAN
Leap Year	21 TISHREI	30 SHVAT	10 SIVAN

7. **"Revere My sanctuary"** (*Vayikra* 19:30)

   If a person speaks or listens to *lashon hara* or *rechilus* in a shul or Beis Midrash, he violates the mitzvah to revere the holy places in which Hashem resides.

8. **"Honor the presence of a Sage"** (*Vayikra* 19:32)

   If a person speaks *lashon hara* or *rechilus* against an elderly person or a Torah scholar in his presence, he violates this mitzvah. (Accepting *lashon hara* spoken against an elderly person in his presence, or a Torah scholar even in his absence, might also violate this mitzvah.)

❧ *Pearls of Life* ❧

If we truly felt the awe of Hashem, Who resides in the shul, we would never allow others to speak words of *lashon hara* there, in violation of Hashem's will.

(*Be'er Mayim Chaim*, positive commandment 7)

❖ ❖ ❖

Just by opening one's mouth, he can forfeit his portion in the World to Come, as our Sages taught: "A person who humiliates his fellow in public has no portion in the World to Come" (*Bava Metzia* 59).

(*Kavod Shamayim*, ch. 2)

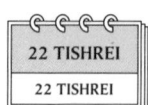 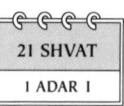 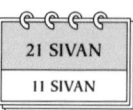

| 22 TISHREI | 21 SHVAT | 21 SIVAN | Daily Calendar |
| 22 TISHREI | 1 ADAR 1 | 11 SIVAN | Leap Year |

9. **"Sanctify [the Kohen]"** (*Vayikra* 21:8).

   The Torah commands us to honor Kohanim. If a person speaks *lashon hara* or *rechilus* against a Kohen in his presence, he violates this mitzvah. (This might also apply even in the Kohen's absence, and even to the listener.)

10. **"Honor your father and mother"** (*Shemos* 20:12).

    a. If a person speaks against his father or mother, he violates this mitzvah, whether or not his parents are present. He also evokes the curse, "Cursed is he who disdains his father or mother." (Accepting *lashon hara* about one's parents might also violate this mitzvah.)

    b. If a person speaks *lashon hara* or *rechilus* against his oldest brother, or against his stepparent, he also violates this mitzvah.

❖ *Pearls of Life* ❖

The Midrash explains that by honoring our parents, we partially repay the debt we owe them for their kindness. One must love them devotedly, just as they love him, and not regard them as an unwanted burden.

(*Sefer Chareidim*, ch. 9, pp. 37–38)

Daily Calendar	23 TISHREI	22 SHVAT	22 SIVAN
Leap Year	23 TISHREI	2 ADAR I	12 SIVAN

11. **"Fear Hashem, your God"** (*Devarim* 10:20).

    When challenged with a difficult mitzvah, we are commanded to arouse our fear of Hashem and remember that He punishes those who disobey Him. If a person freely speaks *lashon hara* or *rechilus*, he transgresses this mitzvah.

12. **Torah study**

    a. Torah study is equivalent to all other mitzvos combined, and there is no limit to its reward. Correspondingly, shirking one's duties in Torah study is equivalent to all other sins combined. A person cannot exempt himself from Torah study with the excuse that he will learn later, since the obligation is incumbent at every moment. If a person uses his precious time to speak *lashon hara* or *rechilus* instead of learning Torah, he violates the mitzvah of Torah study.

    b. If we considered the sin of *bitul Torah* transgressed with each moment of *lashon hara*, in addition to the sin of *lashon hara* itself, we would reach a staggering sum of sins. This is in addition to the other Torah prohibitions and positive commandments detailed above. Therefore, a person must be very careful to refrain from *lashon hara*.

❖ *Pearls of Life* ❖

The mitzvah of Torah study is incumbent every moment. Past learning does not exempt a person from learning now. A person who wastes several hours violates the mitzvah of Torah study with every single moment.

(*Chafetz Chaim*, positive commandment 12)

Introduction to the Laws

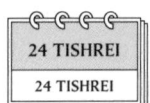 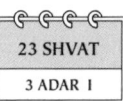 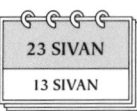

| 24 TISHREI | 23 SHVAT | 23 SIVAN | Daily Calendar |
| 24 TISHREI | 3 ADAR I | 13 SIVAN | Leap Year |

13. **"Distance yourself from falsehood"** (*Shemos* 23:7).

    If even the slightest falsehood is incorporated into one's *lashon hara*, he transgresses this mitzvah. In addition, this is considered "*motzi shem ra* — spreading a false rumor," which carries a punishment far more severe than truthful *lashon hara* or *rechilus*.

14. **"Walk in His ways"** (*Devarim* 28:9).

    If a person regularly speaks *lashon hara* or *rechilus*, he transgresses the mitzvah to emulate Hashem's ways, which are entirely benevolent. Hashem detests slander, even when it is spoken against truly terrible people.

SUMMARY

We have listed here fourteen positive commandments that are likely to be violated by *lashon hara* and *rechilus*. These are in addition to the seventeen prohibitions listed above. If, *chas v'shalom*, a person regularly speaks *lashon hara*, he will certainly violate them all over time.

❧ *Pearls of Life* ❧

In the same area that a *tzaddik* sins, he can appease Hashem and find forgiveness. Thus, if he spoke *lashon hara*, his *teshuvah* involves using his words to help others — by admonishing them and encouraging them in Torah and mitzvah observance, and by making peace between them.

(*Shemiras HaLashon, Zechirah*, ch. 13)

Daily Calendar	25 TISHREI	24 SHVAT	24 SIVAN
Leap Year	25 TISHREI	4 ADAR I	14 SIVAN

THE CURSES INVOLVED IN LASHON HARA

1. **"Cursed is he who strikes his fellow in secret"** (*Devarim* 27:24).

   This curse applies to those who speak against others behind their backs, striking them in secret, as it were.

2. **"Cursed is he who misleads a blind man"** (*Devarim* 27:18).

   This curse applies to those who mislead ignorant people by deliberately offering them bad advice. It also applies to those who encourage others to sin. A person who speaks *lashon hara* is cursed for causing his audience to transgress the prohibition of listening to *lashon hara*.

3. **"Cursed is he who does not uphold the words of the Torah"** (*Devarim* 27:26).

   This curse applies to those who entirely disregard any mitzvah of the Torah. If a person makes no effort to restrain himself from speaking *lashon hara*, he falls into this category.

4. **"Cursed is he who scorns his father and/or mother"** (*Devarim* 27:16).

   If a person speaks *lashon hara* against his father or mother, he evokes this curse.

❖ *Pearls of Life* ❖

If the congregants of just one shul would preserve peace in their community as they should, their merit could bring Mashiach.

(*Shemiras HaLashon* II, end of ch. 7)

Introduction to the Laws

 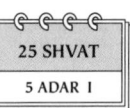 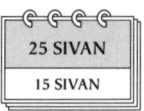

| 26 TISHREI | 25 SHVAT | 25 SIVAN | Daily Calendar |
| 26 TISHREI | 5 ADAR I | 15 SIVAN | Leap Year |

The Laws of *Lashon Hara*

KLAL 1:
The Prohibition of Speaking Lashon Hara, and the Severity of Its Punishment

1. **The definition of *lashon hara***

   a. Speaking disparagingly of another person is considered *lashon hara*, even if the information is entirely true.

   b. If any element of falsehood is added to the *lashon hara*, thereby further degrading the subject, it is considered "*motzi shem ra* — spreading a false rumor," which is a far greater offense.

2. **The *aveiros* involved in *lashon hara***

   A person who speaks *lashon hara* and *rechilus* violates many Torah prohibitions and positive commandments, as listed in the introduction.

❖ *Pearls of Life* ❖

Guarding one's speech entails refraining from any remark that may harm or offend another person, such as *lashon hara*, *rechilus*, controversy, curses, humiliation, and insult.

(*Shemiras HaLashon*, Tevunah, ch. 11)

Daily Calendar	27 TISHREI	26 SHVAT	26 SIVAN
Leap Year	27 TISHREI	6 ADAR I	16 SIVAN

3. **The severe punishment for a *baal lashon hara***

   A person who regularly speaks *lashon hara* is considered a "*baal lashon hara*," whose punishment is far worse.

4. **The punishment for *lashon hara* in this world and the next**

   If a person constantly speaks *lashon hara* and makes no effort to restrain himself, he will be punished in this world, and he has no portion in the World to Come.

> ### ❧ *Pearls of Life* ❧
>
> Rav Chagai taught: *Tzara'as* comes only as a punishment for *lashon hara*. The Sages prove this from Miriam the righteous prophetess, who was struck with *tzara'as* for speaking against her brother Moshe, as the verse states: "Remember what Hashem, your God, did to Miriam on your way out of Egypt."
>
> (*Shemiras HaLashon, Zechirah,* ch. 5)
>
>
>
> During the era of the second Beis HaMikdash, Jerusalem was destroyed only due to the sins of *lashon hara* and senseless hatred (*Yoma* 9b).
>
> (*Kavod Shamayim,* ch. 2)

The Laws of Lashon Hara: Klal 1

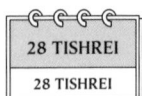 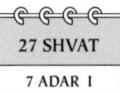 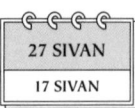

| 28 TISHREI | 27 SHVAT | 27 SIVAN | Daily Calendar |
| 28 TISHREI | 7 ADAR I | 17 SIVAN | Leap Year |

5. *Lashon hara* is forbidden even when solicited

It is forbidden to speak *lashon hara*, even if one is pressured to do so. Even if one's father or rebbe asks him for information that will include the slightest trace of *lashon hara*, it is forbidden to reveal the information.

6. Refraining from *lashon hara* at the expense of one's livelihood

Even if one stands to lose his job for refusing to speak *lashon hara*, and he will then be unable to support his family, he is still forbidden to speak *lashon hara*.

❧ Pearls of Life ❧

Tzara'as upon the walls of a house is not a natural occurrence but a wondrous phenomenon that occurs only among the Jewish people to warn against speaking *lashon hara*. If a person speaks *lashon hara*, first the walls of his house are afflicted with *tzara'as*. If he repents, his house will be purified. If he continues with his wickedness... his skin will be afflicted, and he will become a *metzora*. He will be isolated and publicly disgraced until he ceases to engage in the speech of the wicked, which is marked by mockery and *lashon hara*.

(Rambam, *Tumas Tzara'as* 16:10)

Daily Calendar	29 TISHREI	28 SHVAT	28 SIVAN
Leap Year	29 TISHREI	8 ADAR I	18 SIVAN

7. **Refraining from *lashon hara* at the expense of one's reputation**

   One must refrain from *lashon hara* even if this will cause others to view him as a fool or even hate him.

8. ***Lashon hara* in writing or any other means of communication**

   It is forbidden to write *lashon hara* or to display written material in a way that shows the author in an unfavorable light. It is also forbidden to demean others by non-verbal gestures (such as facial expressions or hand movements).

9. **Including oneself in the *lashon hara***

   Even if the speaker includes himself in the *lashon hara* related against another, and even if he demeans himself first and foremost, it is still forbidden to disgrace others.

❦ *Pearls of Life* ❦

If one's lips and tongue speak words of evil, those words ascend Above.... A proclamation then goes forth to stand away from the evil speech uttered by this person.... The holy *neshamah* will later ascend in shame and terrible anguish, and it will be denied the place it would otherwise have deserved.

(Zohar, *Tazria*)

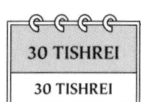 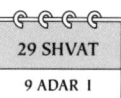 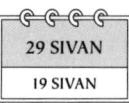

| 30 TISHREI | 29 SHVAT | 29 SIVAN | Daily Calendar |
| 30 TISHREI | 9 ADAR I | 19 SIVAN | Leap Year |

KLAL 2:
Lashon Hara Spoken in the Presence of Three People

1. **Speaking *lashon hara* before one or several people**
   It is forbidden to speak *lashon hara* even to one person. If one speaks to several people, his sin is magnified according to the size of his audience.

2. **Speaking ambiguous *lashon hara* before three people**
   Some comments might be interpreted as derogatory, depending upon the context and manner in which they are spoken. For example, "Food is always being cooked in that person's house" could be interpreted favorably — that the person in question has a large family or invites many guests. It might also be interpreted unfavorably — that he has frivolous parties.

   When such a comment is made in the presence of three or more people, the subject will likely hear of it. The speaker is thus careful to make the comment only in a favorable tone of voice. Therefore it is permitted both for him to speak and for his audience to listen.

❖ Pearls of Life ❖

Although the Torah marks *tzara'as* as the punishment for *lashon hara*, we do not see speakers of *lashon hara* punished with *tzara'as* these days. They are punished with poverty instead, which is likened to *tzara'as*.

(*Shemiras HaLashon*, Zechirah, ch. 6)

3. **Repeating *lashon hara* that was spoken before three people**

   a. If *lashon hara* is spoken in the presence of three people, it will eventually become public knowledge. According to some opinions, a person who heard it spoken in the presence of three may then repeat it in an incidental manner (without intent to spread the *lashon hara*).

   b. Some hold that it is forbidden to repeat it even incidentally, unless the information arises in the course of a different discussion.

4. **Hearsay that the *lashon hara* was spoken before three**

   a. If one knows that *lashon hara* was spoken, but does not know how many people heard it, and he was then told that it was spoken in the presence of three, he may not rely on this to repeat the information, even if he does not say from whom he heard it.

   b. Even if he personally knew that *lashon hara* was spoken, and he was then told that it was spoken in the presence of three, he may not rely on this to repeat the information, unless it has already become public knowledge.

❧ *Pearls of Life* ❧

Speech is the most precious of all human faculties. Therefore one must carefully guard his tongue by practicing the trait of silence. He must treat his words like gold, silver, and precious jewels, which are locked away in a safe in the innermost chamber of his home.

(*Shemiras HaLashon, Tevunah*, ch. 2)

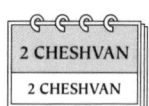	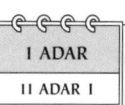	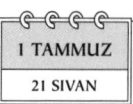	Daily Calendar
2 CHESHVAN / 2 CHESHVAN	1 ADAR / 11 ADAR 1	1 TAMMUZ / 21 SIVAN	Leap Year

5. ***Lashon hara* spoken in the presence of *yirei Shamayim* or relatives**

   The license to repeat *lashon hara* spoken before three people applies only if those who heard it are likely to repeat the information. If even one of the three is a *yirei Shamayim* (God fearing person) who does not speak *lashon hara*, or a friend or relative of the subject, we cannot assume that the information will become public knowledge. Therefore it is forbidden to repeat it.

6. **Repeating *lashon hara* in a different city**

   The above license applies only to repeating the *lashon hara* in the same city where it was spoken before three people. One cannot assume that the information will travel to other cities. Therefore, it is forbidden to repeat it elsewhere.

   If *lashon hara* was spoken in a big city, this restriction might also apply, since news does not travel in a big city as it does in a small town.

❧ *Pearls of Life* ❧

"Why should Hashem be angry over your voice" — with which you spoke *lashon hara*, "and destroy the work of your hands?" (*Koheles* 5:5) — the small amount of Torah you possess.

(*Shemiras HaLashon, Zechirah*, ch. 7)

| Daily Calendar | 3 CHESHVAN | 2 ADAR | 2 TAMMUZ |
| Leap Year | 3 CHESHVAN | 12 ADAR I | 22 SIVAN |

7–8. *Lashon hara* spoken with a warning not to repeat it

a. The license to repeat *lashon hara* spoken before three people does not apply if the speaker warned his audience not to reveal what he said. If one of the three listeners sees that the other two ignored the warning and repeated the *lashon hara* to others, he still may not repeat it, even in an incidental manner.

b. Regardless of how the speaker phrased the warning, it is forbidden to repeat the information to anyone, especially to the subject of the *lashon hara* (since this constitutes *rechilus*).

c. The above license applies only if one person spoke *lashon hara* in the presence of three. If two spoke *lashon hara* in the presence of two others, it is forbidden to repeat it.

⁕ *Pearls of Life* ⁕

If a person lets an evil word leave his lips, spirits of impurity seize that word and use it to defile any words of holiness he may later speak. He thereby loses the merit of his holy words.

(*Shemiras HaLashon, Zechirah*, ch. 7)

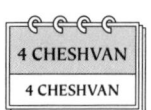 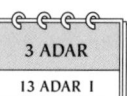 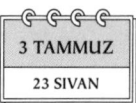

| 4 CHESHVAN | 3 ADAR | 3 TAMMUZ | Daily Calendar |
| 4 CHESHVAN | 13 ADAR I | 23 SIVAN | Leap Year |

9. **Not embellishing *lashon hara***

   a. The license to repeat *lashon hara* spoken before three people allows one only to repeat the *lashon hara* as he heard it spoken. He may not embellish it by adding even one detail, nor may he support the rumor with comments such as "Isn't that just like him?"

   b. Even if it is public knowledge that a certain person misbehaved in his youth or comes from a disreputable family, it is forbidden to speak badly of him if he now behaves properly.

10. **To whom may it be repeated?**

    a. *Lashon hara* spoken in the presence of three may be repeated only to a person who will not immediately believe it to be true. If he will immediately accept it, or might even add words of disdain, it is forbidden under any circumstances to tell him.

    b. In conclusion: In light of these restrictions, the license to repeat *lashon hara* spoken in public is rarely applicable. Furthermore, even if all the conditions are fulfilled, it is unclear whether this license is accepted in halacha (Jewish law). Therefore, one should not rely on this leniency.

❧ *Pearls of Life* ❧

When a person speaks *lashon hara*, he brings sin upon himself and upon his audience. Our Sages tell us that a person who causes another to sin is worse than a murderer, since he robs that person of eternal life in the World to Come.

(*Shemiras HaLashon*, Zechirah, ch. 13)

Daily Calendar	5 CHESHVAN	4 ADAR	4 TAMMUZ
Leap Year	5 CHESHVAN	14 ADAR I	24 SIVAN

11. City council meetings

If a city council agrees on a decision that benefits some people but harms others, no council member may later reveal that he voted against the decision, but his peers outvoted him. This is forbidden whether he reveals it of his own free will or under duress.

❧ *Pearls of Life* ❧

What merit do we have in our small amount of Torah study, if we defile our mouths with words of *lashon hara, rechilus,* mockery, and controversy? How much holiness can rest upon Torah study that comes from a mouth sullied by such sins?

(*Shemiras HaLashon, Zechirah,* ch. 7)

The Torah understands the depths of our nature, and reveals to us that we are indeed capable of guarding our tongues.

(*Chafetz Chaim,* Introduction)

The Laws of Lashon Hara: Klal 2

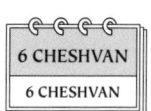 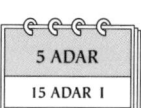 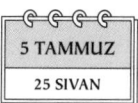

Daily Calendar

Leap Year

12. Mocking a public speaker

a. It is forbidden to mock a public speaker, by claiming that his speech was worthless. Instead, one should approach the speaker privately and advise him how to improve his speeches. Thereby, he fulfills the mitzvah to "Love your neighbor as yourself."

b. Those who mock public speakers, and those who listen to their mockery, violate almost all the positive and prohibitive commandments listed in the introduction to this book. Furthermore, they join the ranks of the "liars, scoffers, and speakers of *lashon hara*," who will not merit to behold the *Shechinah* (*Sotah* 42a). By mocking a Torah lecture, one also discourages Torah observance.

13. Business secrets

a. If a person reveals information about his business before three or more people, he shows that he has no objection to publicizing this information. It is therefore permitted to repeat it (under the guidelines discussed above regarding *lashon hara* spoken in the presence of three; see rules 3–10).

b. Some rule that if a person is told private information that will cause no harm if revealed, he may repeat it. However, he should train himself not to repeat what he has been told, unless he has been given explicit permission. Others are of the opinion that in any case, private information may not be repeated.

Daily Calendar	7 CHESHVAN	6 ADAR	6 TAMMUZ
Leap Year	7 CHESHVAN	16 ADAR I	26 SIVAN

KLAL 3:
Lashon Hara in the Subject's Presence, as a Joke, or without Revealing the Subject's Name

1. **Lashon hara**

   The Torah forbids speaking *lashon hara*, even if it is true, regardless of whether the subject is present. It is forbidden to discuss a person's shortcomings, including his faults in Torah observance. Even if there is no way to judge him favorably, it is still forbidden to speak *lashon hara* of him.

2. **Lashon hara in the subject's presence**

   Some comments might be interpreted as derogatory depending upon their context and the manner in which they are spoken. In the presence of the subject, one would normally make such a comment in a favorable manner. In such a manner, it is permitted even if the subject is not present. However, if one speaks in a negative manner, it is forbidden even if he would have had the audacity to speak this way in the subject's presence.

⁂ *Pearls of Life* ⁂

For four sins, a person is partially punished in this world, while the principal punishment awaits him in the World to Come: idolatry, illicit relations, murder — and *lashon hara* is equivalent to them all.

(*Shemiras HaLashon, Zechirah*, ch. 8, citing *Talmud Yerushalmi*)

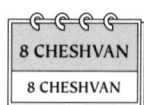 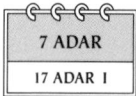 

| 8 CHESHVAN | 7 ADAR | 7 TAMMUZ | Daily Calendar |
| 8 CHESHVAN | 17 ADAR I | 27 SIVAN | Leap Year |

3. **Lashon hara as a joke**

   Even if *lashon hara* is not motivated by hatred, and one has no intention to disgrace his subject, but simply means it as a joke or light banter — it is still forbidden by Torah law.

4. **Concealing the subject's name; causing indirect damage**

   a. *Lashon hara* is forbidden even if one does not state the name of the subject, if his identity can be discerned from the story.

   b. *Lashon hara* is forbidden even if one does not directly disgrace his subject but craftily reveals information that will indirectly cause harm or embarrassment.

❖ *Pearls of Life* ❖

If a person makes no effort to observe a certain mitzvah, he is considered a *mumar* (heretic) in regard to that mitzvah, and his sin is too weighty to bear. Of this the Torah states, "Cursed is he who does not uphold the words of the Torah" (*Devarim* 27:26) — meaning that he does not accept upon himself to observe the entire Torah.

(*Shaarei Teshuvah* 1:6)

Daily Calendar	9 CHESHVAN	8 ADAR	8 TAMMUZ
Leap Year	9 CHESHVAN	18 ADAR I	28 SIVAN

5. **Underhanded** *lashon hara*

    It is forbidden to speak *lashon hara* in an underhanded way, pretending as if he did not realize this was *lashon hara*, or that the action of which he spoke was performed by the subject.

6. **Harmless** *lashon hara*

    a. Even if no harm was caused by one's *lashon hara* — such as if his audience did not believe it — he still transgressed a prohibition, and requires atonement.

    b. Even if one knows no harm will come of his *lashon hara*, it is still forbidden.

❖ *Pearls of Life* ❖

David HaMelech said in Tehillim (34:13): "Who is the man who desires life, loving days to see good? Guard your tongue from evil...." The wise person will resolve to guard his tongue, lest he defile his speech with forbidden words. He will set aside time each day to contemplate whether he controls his speech properly.

(*Chovas HaShemirah*, Introduction)

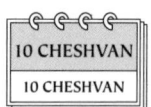 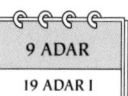 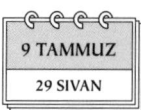

| 10 CHESHVAN | 9 ADAR | 9 TAMMUZ | Daily Calendar |
| 10 CHESHVAN | 19 ADAR I | 29 SIVAN | Leap Year |

7. **Judging favorably**

   Upon witnessing an action of questionable moral or religious virtue, we are required to judge the subject favorably. The degree to which we must tilt the scales in his favor depends upon the subject:

   a. If the subject is known to be a God-fearing person, we must judge him favorably, even if the evidence seems weighted against him.

   b. If the subject is known to be of mediocre religious observance, generally refraining from sin, but occasionally sinning—

       i. If the evidence seems weighted in his favor, or equally balanced, we must judge him favorably.

       ii. Even if the evidence seems weighted against him, it is proper to reserve judgment rather than presume him guilty.

8. ***Lashon hara*** **against the guilty**

   Even when permitted to judge a person unfavorably, we are only allowed to view him as guilty in our estimation. We are not allowed to then speak *lashon hara* of him, unless the conditions discussed in the following chapter are fulfilled.

❖ *Pearls of Life* ❖

We must avoid flattering the wicked. Flatterers are among the four groups of people who will not merit to behold the *Shechinah* (see *Sotah* 42a).

(Be'er Mayim Chaim, prohibition 16)

Daily Calendar	11 CHESHVAN	10 ADAR	10 TAMMUZ
Leap Year	11 CHESHVAN	20 ADAR I	30 SIVAN

KLAL 4:
Lashon Hara regarding Faults in Religious Observance

1. Religious observance

a. It is forbidden to say anything that will disgrace a person, even if it is true, and even if the subject is not present to suffer embarrassment.

b. This includes the misdeeds of his parents or relatives, or misdeeds he himself committed in the past. Even if he recently sinned, it is forbidden to speak *lashon hara* of him, even if he is not present. (Misdeeds *bein adam l'chaveiro* — between man and his fellow — will be discussed in Klal 10).

2. Major or minor misdeeds

It is forbidden to speak of a person's misdeeds, whether he transgresses Torah prohibitions, positive commandments that are widely known and observed, positive commandments that are commonly overlooked (such as Torah study), or even if he just engages in practices deemed improper by the Sages, although not absolutely forbidden.

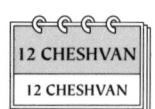 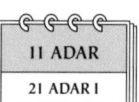 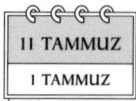

Daily Calendar

Leap Year

3. **An average person who was caught sinning**

   If a person is known to be of average religious observance (generally refraining from sin, but occasionally sinning), even if two witnesses saw him commit the same sin several times, it is forbidden to reveal his sin or even to hate him. He must be judged favorably. Perhaps he sinned inadvertently, he did not know his action was forbidden, or he did not realize the severity of the prohibition.

4. **Intentional sins**

   If he clearly knew the severity of the sin and sinned intentionally:

   a. If he generally refrains from sin, and was caught only once committing this sin in private, it is forbidden to tell even Torah authorities. One must admonish him gently and privately and encourage him to guard himself in the future from the circumstances that led him to sin.

   b. If he is a generally pious Torah scholar, but his *yetzer hara* overcame him this once, it is strictly forbidden to reveal his sin. One must not even think badly of him, since it must be assumed that he has since done *teshuvah*.

❧ Pearls of Life ❧

"One who guards his mouth and tongue guards his soul from suffering" (*Mishlei* 21:23). Suffering in Hebrew is *tzaros*, which is similar to the word *tzara'as*. The Midrash therefore interprets this verse to mean that he guards himself from *tzara'as*, which afflicts the soul and prevents it from entering Hashem's Chamber in Gan Eden.

(*Shemiras HaLashon*, Zechirah, ch. 6)

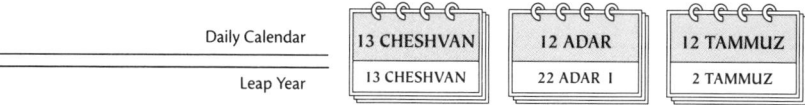

5–6. When admonishment does not suffice

If one is certain that his rebuke will be ignored, and the sinner might repeat his sin, stronger methods must be taken.

a. If two people saw him sin, they should report him to the local Beis Din, which is authorized to punish him and prevent him from sinning again.

b. If only one witness saw him sin, the witness may not report to Beis Din, since the testimony of a single witness is invalid. (Since the testimony is fruitless, it is considered *lashon hara*). Rather, the witness should inform the subject's rabbi or close friend, if they trust him as they would trust two witnesses. The rabbi or friend may then hate and dissociate from the subject, until he repents. However, the rabbi or friend may not repeat the information to anyone else.

 If the rabbi or friend can influence the sinner to repent, it might be permitted to tell them, even if they are apt to repeat the information to someone else.

c. If the sinner's relatives will believe the single witness, he may tell them in order that they may rebuke their relative. In any of the above cases, the witness's intention must be for the sake of Heaven.

❧ *Pearls of Life* ❧

The *Yalkut* (*Korach*) writes that the terrible effects of controversy can be inferred from the words מכה (hit), חרון (anger), לוקה (strike), קללה (curse), and תכלית (annihilation), whose initials spell the word מחלקת (controversy).

(*Shemiras HaLashon, Zechirah*, ch. 15)

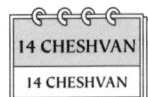	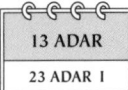		Daily Calendar
14 CHESHVAN	13 ADAR	13 TAMMUZ	
14 CHESHVAN	23 ADAR I	3 TAMMUZ	Leap Year

7. **Degrading the wicked**

   If a person regularly violates a prohibition known by all to be forbidden (such that he was certainly aware of it), one may disgrace him for his sins and speak against him whether or not he is present. However, as long as the sinner is not considered an *apikores* (see Klal 8, rule 5), one must fulfill the following conditions before speaking against him:

   a. One must know firsthand that he has sinned. One may not rely on hearsay, unless the subject is already well known to be a constant sinner.

   b. One must be certain that his misdeeds were truly forbidden.

   c. One must not exaggerate.

   d. One's intention must be for the sake of practical benefit, such as discouraging others from following his evil ways, or encouraging him to repent.

   e. One may not speak against him in secret and flatter him in his presence. Rather, one must speak against him publicly (unless he fears the subject might harm him or instigate a controversy, in which case he may speak against him in private).

   Upon hearing a person accused of wicked deeds, one may not believe the accusation to be true. He may only harbor a doubt, in order to protect himself, until the rumor has been proven either true or false.

   Once a person has been found to be wicked, if he is caught in a morally questionable act, one may not judge him favorably. One must assume the worst and may disgrace him accordingly.

8. **A person who does not comply with the ruling of Beis Din**

   If a person does not comply with the ruling of Beis Din and offers no legitimate excuse, one may speak against him and even record his misdeeds for posterity. However, if he offers an excuse that might be legitimate, it is forbidden to speak against him.

9. **Character flaws**

   It is forbidden to degrade a person for his character flaws, such as arrogance, anger, and the like. Perhaps he has since regretted his behavior and done *teshuvah*. Even if he has not done *teshuvah*, perhaps he does not realize the severity of bad *middos* (character traits). If he knew, perhaps he would better himself. Instead of speaking against him, one should reproach him by explaining the severity of bad *middos*. Thereby, rather than transgressing *lashon hara*, one fulfills the mitzvah of offering admonishment.

10. **Warning others not to learn bad traits**

    If one intends to warn others not to learn from the subject's flaws, it is a mitzvah to speak against him. However, one must clarify to his listeners that he is speaking for a constructive purpose, lest they learn from his example to speak *lashon hara*.

    Even if one did not personally witness the bad traits, he may still guard himself from the subject. He may also warn others to guard themselves, provided that he tells them that he only heard the information, and has no first hand knowledge.

❧ *Pearls of Life* ❧

One who guards his tongue merits *ru'ach hakodesh* (Divine inspiration).

(*Zohar, Chukkas*)

❧   ❧   ❧

If one began to speak and realizes that by concluding his point he will speak *lashon hara*, he must stop in mid-sentence and change the subject.

(*Shemiras HaLashon, Tevunah*, ch. 3)

The Laws of Lashon Hara: Klal 4

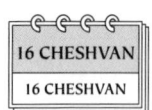 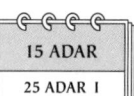 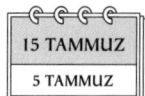

| 16 CHESHVAN | 15 ADAR | 15 TAMMUZ | Daily Calendar |
| 16 CHESHVAN | 25 ADAR I | 5 TAMMUZ | Leap Year |

11. Inquiring about a person for business or *shidduchim*

If one requires information about a potential employee, business partner, or *shidduch* (marital match), it is strongly advisable to inquire about him. However, the following conditions must be fulfilled:

a. One must not ask the subject's competitors or people who seem to dislike him.

b. One must explain the reason he is asking. (Otherwise the person providing negative information commits *lashon hara*.)

c. One must not assume the information to be true. He may only suspect that it might be true, in order to guard himself from harm.

The informant must not exaggerate what he knows to be true (see below, "The Laws of *Rechilus*," Klal 9).

⁕ *Pearls of Life* ⁕

One should not say: "Why should I bother learning the laws of *lashon hara*? Instead I will just accustom myself to remain silent." Often one is required to speak about other people. Therefore, he must learn the laws of what may or may not be said.

(*Shemiras HaLashon, Tevunah*, ch. 2)

Daily Calendar	17 CHESHVAN	16 ADAR	16 TAMMUZ
Leap Year	17 CHESHVAN	26 ADAR I	6 TAMMUZ

12. *Teshuvah* for *lashon hara*

If a person spoke *lashon hara*, but his audience did not believe him, and no disgrace or harm was caused to the subject, he still committed a sin *bein adam l'Makom* (between man and God). To do *teshuvah*, he must regret his deed, confess to Hashem, and resolve never to repeat it.

If his listeners did believe him, and the subject was demeaned in their eyes, then one must first ask forgiveness from his victim. After the victim forgives him, he must do *teshuvah* for the *bein adam l'Makom* aspect, by regretting his deed, confessing to Hashem, and resolving never to repeat it.

In light of this, we are led to understand the great danger of *lashon hara* and how important it is to refrain from it. If a person regularly speaks *lashon hara*, it is almost impossible for him to do *teshuvah*. He could never remember all the people he has spoken against, in order to ask their forgiveness. Even if he does remember some of his victims, he will be ashamed to tell them what he said.

If he speaks against a family, he might harm them for all future generations, for which he will never attain forgiveness.

❧ *Pearls of Life* ❧

By refraining from *lashon hara*, one spares himself the anger of others and causes them to love him and trust him with their secrets. *Middah k'negged middah* (as equal and appropriate reward), no one will ever speak badly of him.

(*Shemiras HaLashon, Zechirah*, ch. 11, citing the Arizal)

In a non leap-year, the following page should also be learned.

The Laws of Lashon Hara: Klal 4

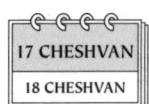 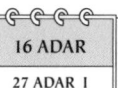 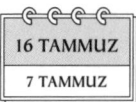

| 17 CHESHVAN | 16 ADAR | 16 TAMMUZ | Daily Calendar |
| 18 CHESHVAN | 27 ADAR I | 7 TAMMUZ | Leap Year |

KLAL 5:
Lashon Hara regarding Faults in Matters Bein Adam L'Chaveiro

In a non leap-year, this page is learned in addition to the previous one.

1. **Disgracing a person for his faults in personal interactions**

   a. It is forbidden to disgrace a person for his faults in matters *bein adam l'chaveiro* (ethical interaction among people), even if the complaint is entirely true. For example, one may not degrade a person who refused to do a favor.

   b. This prohibition applies even if the speaker saw the subject refuse to do a favor, and he knows that the subject was able to do it. If the speaker himself had asked a favor and was refused, it is certainly forbidden to disgrace the subject. Doing so also violates the prohibition of "Do not take revenge" (*Vayikra* 19:18).

⁂ *Pearls of Life* ⁂

Our Sages tell us that most people are guilty of some form of thievery, only a few are guilty of illicit relations, and everyone is guilty of the "dust" of *lashon hara* (*Bava Basra* 165a).

Therefore the Rambam (*Issurei Biah* 22:19, 20) writes that one must make an extra effort to subjugate his *yetzer hara* in these areas.

2. Disgracing a person for his inadequacies

a. It is forbidden to disgrace a person for his lack of intelligence, strength or wealth, or for any other inadequacy. If one's description of these faults is exaggerated or even partly untrue, he is considered a spreader of false rumors (*motzi shem ra*), whose sin is far worse.

b. Insulting a person's intelligence is the worst offense. If the subject is not yet married, it will damage his prospects for *shidduchim*. If he is a tradesman, it will damage his business. If he is a *rav*, it will damage his standing in the eyes of the community and may cost him his job. Insulting the *rav*'s intelligence also dishonors the Torah and its students.

⸙ *Pearls of Life* ⸙

One should refrain from bickering over monetary matters, since he may lose his temper and say forbidden words that dishonor Hashem. If a person forgives injury, trusts Hashem, and prays that his loss be restored, Hashem will protect him and provide for his worldly needs.

(*Shemiras HaLashon, Tevunah*, ch. 11)

In a non-leap year, the following page should also be learned.

The Laws of Lashon Hara: Klal 5

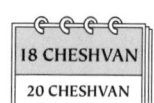 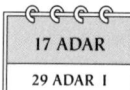 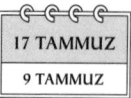

| Daily Calendar |
| Leap Year |

18 CHESHVAN / 20 CHESHVAN — 17 ADAR / 29 ADAR I — 17 TAMMUZ / 9 TAMMUZ

In a non leap-year, this page is learned in addition to the previous one.

3. Disgracing a person for his inadequacies (continued)

a. The *yetzer hara* would have us believe that only insulting a person for his actions is considered *lashon hara*, but insulting him for his inadequacies is not. In fact, this is the worst form of *lashon hara*, since one's intention is usually just to disgrace the subject. Furthermore, people are more prone to believe this kind of slander.

b. However, if discussing a person's inadequacies can defuse an argument, it is a mitzvah to do so. For example, if Reuven hates Shimon, believing he purposely offended him, it is a mitzvah to convince Reuven that Shimon acted out of foolishness, not harmful intent.

4. Disgracing a person for his inadequacy in Torah

If a community considers a certain person to be knowledgeable in Torah, it is forbidden to tell them that his Torah knowledge is limited. Even if it is true, one may not say so without sufficient reason, as this could cause him embarrassment or even loss of livelihood. However, if a community is considering electing a certain person to a rabbinical position based on a false impression of his Torah knowledge, it is permitted to reveal the truth, in accordance with the conditions listed below in "The Laws of *Rechilus*," Klal 9.

❖ *Pearls of Life* ❖

The Torah forbids even a modicum of falsehood, especially in regard to *lashon hara*, where even a slight alteration of facts can change the whole story.

(Chafetz Chaim, Laws of *Lashon Hara*, ch. 1;
Be'er Mayim Chaim 2)

| Daily Calendar | 19 CHESHVAN | 18 ADAR | 18 TAMMUZ |
| Leap Year | 21 CHESHVAN | 30 ADAR I | 10 TAMMUZ |

5. Disgracing a person for his lack of strength or wealth

By declaring someone physically weak, one can cause him harm. For example, if he is a laborer who requires physical strength, people will be reluctant to hire him. Similarly, if one declares a person poor, or not as wealthy as he seems, people will be reluctant to do business with him. In these and similar cases, by speaking *lashon hara*, one can cause the subject pain and anguish and even destroy his livelihood.

However, if practical benefit can be gained by revealing this information, it is permitted to do so, in accordance with the conditions set forth below in "The Laws of *Rechilus*," Klal 9.

6. *Lashon hara* depends upon the subject

Certain comments may or may not be considered *lashon hara*, depending upon the subject. The same comment may compliment one person but insult another. For example:

a. Saying that someone learns Torah for three of four hours a day. When said about a working person, this is a great compliment. When said about a yeshiva student, it is an insult.

b. Saying that someone spends a certain amount of money for his Shabbos needs or charity. When said about a person of limited means, this may be a compliment. When said about a rich person, it may be an insult, since he could spend more.

The general rule one must always remember, is that any comment that could cause personal or monetary harm, anguish or fear, is considered *lashon hara*.

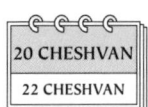 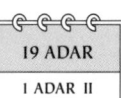 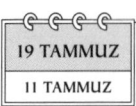

| 20 CHESHVAN | 19 ADAR | 19 TAMMUZ | Daily Calendar |
| 22 CHESHVAN | I ADAR II | II TAMMUZ | Leap Year |

7. **Degrading a person's possessions**

    Degrading someone's possessions is also considered *lashon hara*. For example, if a jealous merchant disparages his competitor's wares, this is considered *lashon hara*.

8. **Two people who speak *lashon hara***

    If two people speak *lashon hara* together, their sin if far worse, since their audience is more likely to believe them. If one person has already revealed a piece of *lashon hara*, and a second person repeats it, the second person also violates the prohibition of *lashon hara*.

⸙ Pearls of Life ⸙

If a person does not guard his tongue from forbidden speech, he brings poverty upon himself, *chas v'shalom*. The author of *Sefer HaKaneh* was once asked by his students: If *lashon hara* causes *tzara'as*, why isn't the great majority of Klal Yisrael afflicted with it? He answered that we are instead afflicted with poverty, which is equated with *tzara'as*.

(*Kavod Shamayim*, ch. 2)

Daily Calendar	21 CHESHVAN	20 ADAR	20 TAMMUZ
Leap Year	23 CHESHVAN	2 ADAR II	12 TAMMUZ

KLAL 6:
Listening to and Believing Lashon Hara

1. **Accepting *lashon hara***

   a. The Torah forbids us to accept *lashon hara*. This means that we must not believe *lashon hara* to be true, whether it regards matters *bein adam l'Makom* (religious observance) or *bein adam l'chaveiro* (ethical interaction among people).

   b. Often, it is not necessary to presume that the person who told *lashon hara* is lying. The story may be true, but the subject can still be judged favorably. However, if according to the story there is no way to judge the subject favorably, then one must not believe the story at all.

2. **Listening to *lashon hara***

   a. The Torah forbids us to listen to *lashon hara*, even if we are resolved not to believe it. However, if the story has practical relevance — for example, if one is considering a *shidduch* or a business deal with the subject — he may listen in order to protect himself, provided that he does not believe for certain that it is true. He may only take the necessary precautions to protect himself.

   b. One may also listen to the story in order to help others, e.g., to admonish the subject. In any such case, it is forbidden to believe for certain that the story is true.

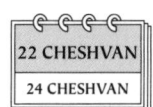 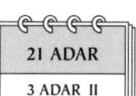 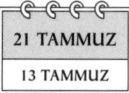

22 CHESHVAN / 24 CHESHVAN	
21 ADAR / 3 ADAR II	
21 TAMMUZ / 13 TAMMUZ	

Daily Calendar

Leap Year

3. **Avoiding *lashon hara***

If someone wishes to speak *lashon hara*, the listener should ask if the information has any practical relevance to himself, or if he will be able to correct the situation by admonishing the subject. If the answer is yes, then he may listen to the story, but he may not believe it is true. If he sees no practical benefit, he may not even listen.

When the speaker encounters such a response, or an expression of disfavor, he will be discouraged from speaking *lashon hara* again in the future.

4. **When is it a mitzvah to listen to *lashon hara*?**

   a. If there is a benefit to listening to *lashon hara*, such as being able to disprove the story or show how to judge the subject favorably, then it is a mitzvah to listen. The listener will thereby be able to vindicate the subject before the speaker and the audience and prevent the speaker from telling others. (In such cases where it is permitted to listen to *lashon hara*, one may not assume for certain that the story is true. He may only take the necessary precautions to guard himself from harm.)

   b. If one listened to *lashon hara*, he can retroactively correct his sin by immediately showing the speaker how the subject can be judged favorably. He must attempt to dissuade the speaker from his bad impression of the subject.

   However, if one knows that the more he attempts to vindicate the subject, the more the speaker will degrade him, it is best to remain silent. After the speaker leaves, one should attempt to convince the rest of the audience not to accept the *lashon hara*.

Daily Calendar	23 CHESHVAN	22 ADAR	22 TAMMUZ
Leap Year	25 CHESHVAN	4 ADAR II	14 TAMMUZ

5. If one finds himself among gossipers

a. If one finds himself amongst a group of people speaking *lashon hara*, and rebuking them would be futile, he must leave their company if possible, or plug his ears.

b. If he cannot leave, and he is too embarrassed to plug his ears, then in order to observe the Torah prohibition against listening to *lashon hara*, he must fulfill three conditions:

   i. He must resolve not to believe the *lashon hara*.

   ii. He must not enjoy hearing it.

   iii. He must not say anything or show any expression that implies his assent. If possible, he should show them an expression of disfavor.

6. Joining a group of gossipers

a. If one joins a group of people speaking *lashon hara*, fails to leave when they begin speaking *lashon hara* (when he is able to do so), or joins a group known for its *lashon hara*, he is considered a sinner just as they are, even if he does not join or enjoy their conversation.

b. If he intentionally joins them in order to hear *lashon hara*, his sin is far worse. He will be inscribed Above as a wicked person and a *baal lashon hara*.

❧ *Pearls of Life* ❧

The Midrash says that Hashem will save us from all forms of misfortune, since He wants only to judge us favorably. However, this is on condition that the Satan does not wage his accusations against us. When people speak *lashon hara*, they invite the Satan to speak against them.

(*Zechor L'Miriam* ch. 3)

The Laws of Lashon Hara: Klal 6

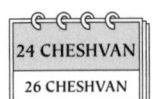 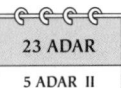 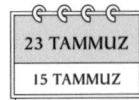

| 24 CHESHVAN | 23 ADAR | 23 TAMMUZ | Daily Calendar |
| 26 CHESHVAN | 5 ADAR II | 15 TAMMUZ | Leap Year |

7. **Listening to an unfavorable judgment**

   If one hears *lashon hara* that he knows to be true, but the subject could have been judged favorably, he may not accept the speaker's unfavorable judgment. If he does so, he transgresses the prohibition against accepting *lashon hara*, in addition to the commandment to "Judge your fellow with righteousness" (*Vayikra* 19:15). The obligation to judge others favorably applies even if their religious observance is mediocre.

8. **A God-fearing person who could be judged favorably**

   a. If *lashon hara* is told about a God-fearing person (whom we are especially obligated to judge favorably), and one agrees with the speaker's unfavorable judgment — this is certainly considered accepting *lashon hara*.

   b. If a person lost a case in Beis Din, and he proceeds to slander the court for ruling against him, one should attempt to calm him, and refute his complaints against Beis Din. If one is unsuccessful, he should at least not believe the slander. Rather, he must judge the Beis Din favorably. Otherwise, he is guilty of accepting *lashon hara*.

⁌ *Pearls of Life* ⁌

No organ is as self-destructive as the mouth. Every forbidden word creates a prosecuting angel. In just one hour, hundreds of words of *lashon hara* and *rechilus* can be spoken. Conversely, if a person speaks as he should, his speech will be the greatest cause of his fortune and success.

(*Shemiras HaLashon* II, ch. 30)

Daily Calendar	25 CHESHVAN	24 ADAR	24 TAMMUZ
Leap Year	27 CHESHVAN	6 ADAR II	16 TAMMUZ

9. Whatever may not be spoken may not be believed

a. Anything that may not be spoken, may not be believed. Therefore, if a person is degraded for his parents' deeds, for his own past deeds (though he now behaves properly), or for his lack of intelligence, one may not believe it.

b. It is similarly forbidden to believe written *lashon hara*.

10. Suspecting *lashon hara* to be true

a. Although the Torah forbids believing *lashon hara*, or even suspecting it to be true, one must take the necessary precautions to protect himself or others from harm. If there is no practical relevance to the *lashon hara*, this leniency does not apply.

b. Even in such a case, we are still obligated to grant the suspect all the privileges he deserves as a Jew, including giving him tzedakah and returning his lost objects. This is true even if, according to the claims against him, he has left the fold of Klal Yisrael.

❧ *Pearls of Life* ❧

If we were asked to donate money to rebuild the Beis HaMikdash, how proud we would be to have this opportunity. We would donate to the best of our ability, in order to have a portion in this great merit. Yet we do not need money to build the Beis HaMikdash. We need only to refrain from *lashon hara* and senseless hatred, and promote peace instead. How honored will such a person be in the World to Come, when it will be made known that his merit caused the Beis HaMikdash to be rebuilt.

(*Shemiras HaLashon* II, end of ch. 7)

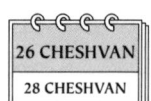 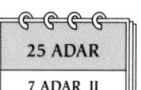 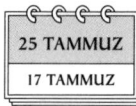

| 26 CHESHVAN | 25 ADAR | 25 TAMMUZ | Daily Calendar |
| 28 CHESHVAN | 7 ADAR II | 17 TAMMUZ | Leap Year |

11. Acting upon *lashon hara*

a. If a person hears *lashon hara*, he must not act upon it to cause any damage or disgrace to the subject. One may not even hate him on the basis of *lashon hara*.

b. On the basis of *lashon hara*, one may not neglect any obligation toward the subject. For example, if an employee has been accused of theft, his employer may not withhold his salary, unless the matter has been proven true. Similarly, if a poor man collects tzedakah, one may not refuse to give him on the basis of *lashon hara* that he is deceiving his patrons. (Although one may suspect the *lashon hara* to be true in order to protect himself, he may not rely on it to absolve himself of the obligation to give tzedakah.)

12. *Teshuvah* for accepting *lashon hara*

a. If one has accepted *lashon hara* but has not repeated it to others, his atonement involves:

   i. Resolving no longer to believe the story he had accepted.

   ii. Resolving never again to accept *lashon hara*.

   iii. Confessing to Hashem that he sinned by accepting *lashon hara*.

b. If he repeated the *lashon hara* to others, he has no atonement until he appeases the person he spoke against, or convinces the people he told not to believe his *lashon hara*. He must also follow the three steps outlined above.

Daily Calendar —  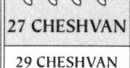 27 CHESHVAN 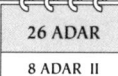 26 ADAR 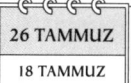 26 TAMMUZ
Leap Year — 29 CHESHVAN | 8 ADAR II | 18 TAMMUZ

KLAL 7:
Details of the Laws of Accepting Lashon Hara

1. **_Lashon hara_ spoken before a large audience**

   Even if *lashon hara* was spoken before a large audience, one may not presume the information to be true. One may only take precautions and investigate the matter further. If he finds it to be true, he must rebuke the subject.

2. **_Lashon hara_ spoken in the subject's presence**

   a. Even if *lashon hara* was spoken in the presence of the subject, one may not rely on this to assume that it is true. All the more so, one may not believe it to be true, simply because the speaker claims he *would* have said it in the subject's presence.

   b. Even if the subject usually objects when he hears something he dislikes, and in this case he did not deny the accusation, this is still not considered a confession, and one may not believe it to be true.

When Cheshvan has only twenty-nine days, the pages for the 29th and 30th are both learned on the 29th.

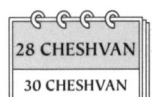 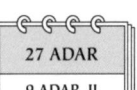 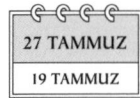

| 28 CHESHVAN | 27 ADAR | 27 TAMMUZ | Daily Calendar |
| 30 CHESHVAN | 9 ADAR II | 19 TAMMUZ | Leap Year |

3. ***Lashon hara* heard from several people**

   Even if one heard the same *lashon hara* from several people, it is still forbidden to believe it. However, one may suspect it to be true in order to protect himself, even if he heard it from only one person.

4. **Rumors**

   a. One may not believe a rumor that a person did or said something wrong. One may only suspect it to be true in order to guard himself from harm, until the matter is clarified.

   b. As discussed above in Klal 2, according to some opinions, and under certain circumstances, one may repeat *lashon hara* that has already become public knowledge, provided that his intention is not to spread the rumor. (See Klal 2, rule 3.)

⸫ *Pearls of Life* ⸫

The sin of accepting *lashon hara* begins with the ears. Through the ears, *lashon hara* enters and defiles the heart, if one believes it to be true. Therefore, the ears are the first to be punished in Gehinnom.

(*Shemiras HaLashon*, Zechirah, ch. 14)

5. **Accepting *lashon hara* about a wicked person**

   a. If a person is known to be wicked, having repeatedly and intentionally violated prohibitions that are familiar to all, one may accept *lashon hara* spoken against him. This holds true even regarding sins he has not been known to commit.

   b. If a rumor circulates for a day and a half that a person committed an act known to be forbidden, and he has no enemies in the city who could have invented the rumor, it is unclear whether one may rely on this rumor to disgrace him, or whether one may believe it altogether.

6. **When the speaker includes himself in his *lashon hara***

   If a person speaks *lashon hara* about himself and others, one may believe it only regarding the speaker, but not regarding others.

⁂ *Pearls of Life* ⁂

One reason a person must dissociate from the wicked is that he will be punished for hearing their constant *lashon hara* and failing to rebuke them.

(Shaarei Teshuvah, ch. 3, 197)

When Cheshvan has only twenty-nine days, the pages for the 29th and 30th are both learned on the 29th.

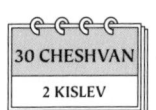 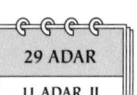 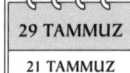

| 30 CHESHVAN | 29 ADAR | 29 TAMMUZ | Daily Calendar |
| 2 KISLEV | 11 ADAR II | 21 TAMMUZ | Leap Year |

7–8. Accepting *lashon hara* from someone as trustworthy as two witnesses

a. Even if one hears *lashon hara* from someone as trustworthy as two witnesses, it is still forbidden to believe him, since he had no permission to speak the *lashon hara*.

b. If someone as trustworthy as two witnesses speaks *lashon hara* for a permitted, constructive purpose, such as telling the subject's rabbi in order that he may rebuke him, then one may believe it, on the following conditions:

   i. The speaker saw the incident himself.

   ii. There is no way to judge the subject favorably.

   iii. One may believe it only in order to hate the subject and dissociate from him until he repents. One may not repeat the *lashon hara* to others, cause the subject monetary loss, or physically harm him.

c. It seems that no one today is as trustworthy as two witnesses. Therefore, one may never assume *lashon hara* to be true. One may only suspect that it might be true, in order to protect himself.

❧ *Pearls of Life* ❧

The Gemara states that any generation in which the Beis HaMikdash is not rebuilt is considered as if the Beis HaMikdash was then destroyed (*Talmud Yerushalmi, Yoma* 5a). By speaking *lashon hara*, one participates in the destruction of the Beis HaMikdash of his own generation.

(*Kavod Shamayim*, ch. 1)

9. **Accepting *lashon hara* spoken innocently ('*masiach l'fi tumo*')**

   a. "*Masiach l'fi tumo*" is when a person relates an incident that portrays another in a negative light, but clearly had no intention of degrading him or arousing controversy.

   b. It is unclear from the Gemara whether such *lashon hara* may be believed. Even if it may be believed, many conditions must be fulfilled. Therefore, in practice one should not accept or even listen to *lashon hara* spoken *l'fi tumo*, even if he does not intend to act upon it.

❧ *Pearls of Life* ❧

The Tanna Rebbe Eliezer HaGadol wrote in his ethical will: "My son, do not sit among a group of slanderers. When their words ascend Above, they are recorded in a ledger, and all who were present are recorded together as a 'society of evil-doers.'"

(*Shemiras HaLashon, Zechirah*, ch. 13)

❧ ❧ ❧

The *yetzer hara* has a ruse by which it beguiles even a righteous person. It need only plant thoughts of anger and belligerence in his heart. Then, even the most crooked road will seem straight in his eyes. The *yetzer hara* will be able to show him many justifications for forbidden behavior.

(*Shemiras HaLashon, Zechirah*, ch. 15)

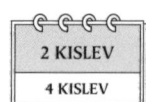 2 KISLEV / 4 KISLEV
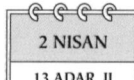 2 NISAN / 13 ADAR II
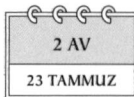 2 AV / 23 TAMMUZ

Daily Calendar
Leap Year

10. Accepting *lashon hara* based on circumstantial evidence

If circumstantial evidence supports the *lashon hara*, it may be believed, provided that the information serves a constructive purpose, such as leading the listener to dissociate from a person who has been proven wicked. If the *lashon hara* entails merely degrading a person for his insufficiencies, one may not accept it, even on the basis of evidence.

Furthermore, even if the evidence supports the facts, one must judge the subject favorably, if he is of at least mediocre religious observance.

Before accepting *lashon hara* on the basis of circumstantial evidence, one must verify that the evidence is conclusive. (The *yetzer hara* leads people to false conclusions, and one must not be quick to judge). One must also fulfill the conditions outlined in the following pages.

❖ *Pearls of Life* ❖

The Rambam writes in his ethical will: "The prophets have prophesied, and the wise men have expounded the great damage caused by controversy, yet they have not succeeded in portraying the full extent of its true evil."

(*Shemiras HaLashon, Zechira* ch. 15)

In a non leap-year, the following page should also be learned.

In a non leap-year, this page is learned in addition to the previous one.

11. Conditions for accepting *lashon hara* on the basis of circumstantial evidence

a. Circumstantial evidence is valid only if it is directly relevant to the case at hand.

b. One must be personally acquainted with the evidence. If he heard of the evidence from someone else, it is invalid.

12. For what ends circumstantial evidence may be employed

a. Even if the circumstantial evidence is conclusive, one may rely on it only to accept the *lashon hara* as true, not to repeat it to others or cause the subject monetary loss or physical harm.

b. However, if circumstantial evidence indicates that the subject has harmed someone, he may tell others and enlist their help in repairing the damage.

⁂ Pearls of Life ⁂

Participating in controversy is so severe that it can be punished by lashes.

(*Shemiras HaLashon, Zechirah*, ch. 15)

It has been tried and proven that refraining from *lashon hara* is difficult only for a few weeks, until one has become accustomed to this good habit.

(*Shemiras HaLashon, Tevunah*, ch. 3)

 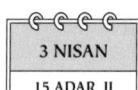 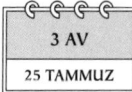

| 3 KISLEV | 3 NISAN | 3 AV | Daily Calendar |
| 6 KISLEV | 15 ADAR II | 25 TAMMUZ | Leap Year |

13. Circumstantial evidence in Beis Din

a. If necessary, Beis Din may force a person to confess. For example, if someone claims that the defendant stole from him, and offers conclusive, circumstantial evidence, Beis Din may beat the defendant into confessing. This is true only if the Beis Din saw the evidence themselves, or heard of it from two witnesses.

b. However, a private individual may not rely on circumstantial evidence to physically harm the suspect, nor may Beis Din rely on it, if they have no knowledge of the evidence other than the claimant's word.

14. Not relying on the claimant's word

Some mistakenly assume that if they merely suspect a person of stealing from them, they may claim before the city council that they have circumstantial evidence. The council unjustly relies on this claim, to beat or otherwise punish the suspect into confession. It is a grave sin to do so.

❖ Pearls of Life ❖

The Satan plagues people who participate in controversy.

(*Gittin* 52)

❖   ❖   ❖

Our Sages tell us that in three notable instances, the Holy One Blessed Be He forgave idolatry, but He did not forgive controversy.

(*Shemiras HaLashon, Zechirah*, ch. 15)

Daily Calendar	4 KISLEV	4 NISAN	4 AV
Leap Year	7 KISLEV	16 ADAR II	26 TAMMUZ

KLAL 8:
The Subject and Audience of Lashon Hara

1. **The speaker**

    Lashon hara is forbidden regardless of whether the speaker is a man or a woman, and whether he/she is a relative of the subject or not.

2. **The subject**

    It is also forbidden regardless of whether the subject is a man or a woman. It is forbidden to speak *lashon hara* about one's spouse or in-laws (unless his intention is constructive, and his story is entirely true).

❃ *Pearls of Life* ❃

The Tosefta states that for three sins a person is partially punished in this world, while his principal punishment awaits him in the World to Come: idolatry, illicit relations, and murder. Yet the punishment for *lashon hara* is equivalent to them all.

For this reason alone, a person must carefully guard himself from this terrible trait. He should consider that all the misfortune he suffers throughout his life is only the "interest" on his punishment for *lashon hara*, but the "principal" still awaits him in the World to Come.

(*Kavod Shamayim*, ch. 1)

 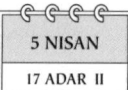 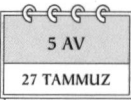

| 5 KISLEV | 5 NISAN | 5 AV | Daily Calendar |
| 8 KISLEV | 17 ADAR II | 27 TAMMUZ | Leap Year |

3. *Lashon hara* about a child

a. It is forbidden to speak *lashon hara* about a child if it could cause him harm or distress.

b. If one's intention is to prevent the child from mischief, or to guide him on the proper path, it is permissible to speak *lashon hara* about him. However, one must personally know that the information is true. One must also consider the outcome of his words. He might create a bad reputation for the child, which might eventually lead to his abandoning Torah observance.

4. *Lashon hara* about Torah scholars and ignoramuses

a. It is forbidden to speak *lashon hara* about any person, whether he is an *am ha'aretz* (ignoramus in Torah matters) or a Torah scholar. However, the punishment for speaking against a Torah scholar is far more severe.

b. The *yetzer hara* would have us believe that there are no true Torah scholars today. This is not so. A Torah scholar is judged relative to his generation. If he toils in Torah and can issue halachic rulings, he is considered a Torah scholar. It is a terrible sin to disgrace him, whether he is present or absent. A person who does so is liable for *niddui* (excommunication by Torah law). It is even worse to disgrace the city's rabbi.

❧ *Pearls of Life* ❧

Our Sages tell us: If there is controversy in a home, it will eventually be destroyed. If there is controversy in a shul, it will eventually be disbanded. If there is controversy in a city, there will be bloodshed in the city.

(*Shemiras HaLashon, Zechirah*, ch. 15)

Daily Calendar	6 KISLEV	6 NISAN	6 AV
Leap Year	9 KISLEV	18 ADAR II	28 TAMMUZ

5–6. *Lashon hara* about *apikorsim*

a. It is a mitzvah to disgrace known *apikorsim* (heretics), both in their presence and in their absence, for any disdainful matter heard or seen of them. (An *apikores* is one who denies the Written or Oral Torah. If he denies that even one established Torah precept is from Hashem, he is considered an *apikores*.)

b. A person may be regarded as an *apikores* only if one personally heard words of heresy from him, or if he has been firmly established in the city as a known *apikores*. One may not rely on hearsay to presume someone an *apikores*, and on this basis speak *lashon hara* about him. One may not even believe this hearsay to be true. He may only take defensive measures to protect himself, and privately warn others not to associate with him until the matter is clarified.

❧ Pearls of Life ❧

One who disgraces a Torah scholar is subject to the admonishment from the Torah, "For he has disgraced the word of Hashem... he will be cut off, and his sin will be upon him" (*Bemidbar* 15:31). There is no cure for the punishment that will befall him.

(*Shemiras HaLashon, Zechirah,* ch. 16)

In a non leap-year, the following page should also be learned.

  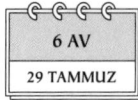

Daily Calendar

Leap Year

In a non leap-year, this page is learned in addition to the previous one.

7. *Lashon hara* against the wicked

   a. If a person is known without doubt to be wicked, based on incessant rumors that he violates well-known prohibitions (even if only minor ones), it is permitted to speak and accept *lashon hara* about him.

   b. However, the following conditions must be fulfilled:

   i. One's intention must be for the sake of Heaven, to distance people from the wicked and perhaps even influence them to repent. One must not enjoy discussing *lashon hara* or speak out of personal hatred.

   ii. One may not exaggerate.

   iii. One may not speak against the subject secretly, unless he fears vengeance or wishes to avoid controversy.

⁕ *Pearls of Life* ⁕

People search for *segulos* (supernatural remedies) and ask Torah leaders for their blessing for a comfortable livelihood.... If they would ask my advice, I would tell them to be extremely careful not to speak *lashon hara*, steal, deceive or harm others. Then they would receive the blessing, "Blessed is he who does not strike his fellow in secret," to which the entire Jewish people answered, "Amen." This blessing will surely be fulfilled.

(*Shemiras HaLashon* II, end of ch. 9)

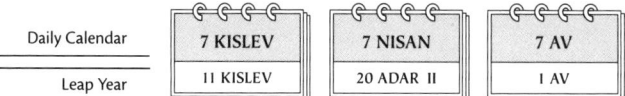

Daily Calendar	7 KISLEV	7 NISAN	7 AV
Leap Year	11 KISLEV	20 ADAR II	1 AV

8. *Lashon hara* against instigators of controversy

Some hold that *lashon hara* may be spoken against those who instigate controversy, if it will help others realize that the instigators are wrong and will ultimately halt the controversy. Otherwise it is forbidden.

The following conditions must also be fulfilled:

a. One must know firsthand that the subject instigated controversy. One may not rely on hearsay, unless it has been proven to be true. Caution must be taken in judging who is considered a *"baal machlokes* — instigator of controversy" according to Torah standards.

b. One's intent must be to halt the controversy, and not out of personal hatred.

c. Speaking *lashon hara* must be the only way to halt the controversy. If one can privately rebuke the instigators, he must do so instead.

9. *Lashon hara* against the deceased

It is forbidden to disgrace the deceased, even if they were ignoramuses in Torah, and certainly if they were Torah scholars. All the more so, one may not mock the Torah teachings of the deceased.

❧ *Pearls of Life* ❧

By speaking *lashon hara*, one draws upon himself harsh judgment from Heaven.

(*Kavod Shamayim*, ch. 2)

The Laws of Lashon Hara: Klal 8

 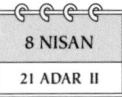 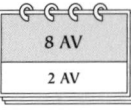

| 8 KISLEV | 8 NISAN | 8 AV | Daily Calendar |
| 12 KISLEV | 21 ADAR II | 2 AV | Leap Year |

10. Speaking *lashon hara* to one's own relatives

a. One may not speak *lashon hara* even to his own relatives, including his spouse.

b. One may tell his spouse *lashon hara* for a constructive purpose. For example, if a woman manages a store, her husband may tell her that certain people are untrustworthy, and she should not sell to them on credit. Such information may also be told to one's business partner.

c. If one has no personal knowledge that they are untrustworthy, having only heard this from others, he may still warn his wife to be cautious, provided that he makes it clear that he does not presume them to be guilty. He may only say, "I have heard stories about them, so be careful."

d. Many unwisely tell their wives everything that happens to them in their social circles, including their arguments, and the insults they suffer. In addition to violating the prohibition against *lashon hara*, one also fuels these controversies by dragging his wife into them. Furthermore, he will only lose his wife's esteem by revealing that he is not respected in his social group. Therefore, one should be very careful never to relate such matters to his wife.

11. Speaking *lashon hara* to the subject's relatives

It is forbidden to speak *lashon hara*, even to the subject's relatives. For this reason, one may not tell his parents *lashon hara* about his siblings. Even if one's intention is for the relative to rebuke the subject, it is still forbidden, if one could have personally rebuked him instead.

Daily Calendar	9 KISLEV	9 NISAN	9 AV
Leap Year	13 KISLEV	22 ADAR II	3 AV

12. *Lashon hara* spoken to a Gentile

a. It is much worse to speak *lashon hara* to a Gentile than to a Jew.

b. If one provides a Gentile with incriminating evidence about a Jew, his sin is too weighty to bear. He takes on the status of an *apikores*, whose punishment will continue even after Gehinnom ceases. It is considered as if he has raised his hand against the holy Torah. Therefore, one must be extremely careful not to take any part in such matters.

❧ *Pearls of Life* ❧

Rebbe Alexandri once called out, "Who wants life?" A large crowd gathered around him. "We want life!" the people said. He then quoted to them the verse "Who is the man who desires life, loving days to see good? Guard your tongue from evil..." (*Tehillim* 34:13).

(*Avodah Zarah* 19b)

One should avoid sitting among groups of people engaged in idle chatter. Thereby, he protects himself from severe sins, including *lashon hara*, *rechilus*, mockery, humiliating others, and so on.

(*Chovas HaShemirah*, ch. 14)

The Laws of Lashon Hara: Klal 8

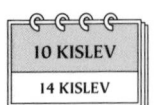 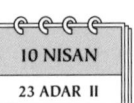 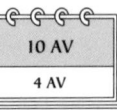

| 10 KISLEV | 10 NISAN | 10 AV | Daily Calendar |
| 14 KISLEV | 23 ADAR II | 4 AV | Leap Year |

13. Accepting *lashon hara*

It is forbidden to believe *lashon hara* about any Jew, with the exception of *apikorsim* — of whom it is permitted to accept *lashon hara*.

14. Accepting *lashon hara* from one's parents

   a. It is forbidden to accept *lashon hara* even from one's parents or other relatives.

   b. If one hears his parents speaking *lashon hara*, he must respectfully stop them in order to spare them punishment. He should not chastise them for violating the sin of *lashon hara*. Rather, he should politely defend the subject of their *lashon hara*, thus preventing them from speaking against him.

   c. One must constantly caution his family against *lashon hara*. In a pleasant manner, he should remind them of the punishment for speaking and accepting *lashon hara* and the reward for refraining.

   d. The behavior of a family usually mirrors that of the head of the household. Therefore, a father must always be careful to set a good example. If his family hears him speak badly of others, he will be unable to prevent them from doing the same. By setting a good example for his family, one will be blessed both in this world and the next.

∻ *Pearls of Life* ∻

Someone who publicly embarrasses another person has no portion in the World to Come.

(*Bava Metzia* 59a)

Daily Calendar	11 KISLEV	11 NISAN	11 AV
Leap Year	15 KISLEV	24 ADAR II	5 AV

KLAL 9:
Avak Lashon Hara

1. ***Avak lashon hara***
   a. It is forbidden to say things that may cause others to speak *lashon hara*. Such remarks are called "*avak lashon hara* — the 'dust' of *lashon hara*." For example, one may not say, "Let's not talk about him. I don't want to say what happened." This might raise others' interest, and prompt them to speak of him.
   b. By praising a person before his enemies, one causes them to refute the praises, and speak against him. This is also considered *avak lashon hara*. For this reason, if one suspects that Reuven is not on good terms with Shimon, one may not mention Shimon in his presence.
   c. One may not excessively praise someone, even if the subject has no enemies in the audience. (Amidst the praises, the speaker will likely also mention some deficiencies.)
   d. Even if the praise is not excessive, it may still be forbidden. For example, one may not praise someone for certain traits in a way that implies his deficiency in others.

2. **Praising someone in public**
   a. It is forbidden to praise someone in public, even if he has no enemies in the audience, as one of the listeners might respond by speaking *lashon hara* about the subject.
   b. If one knows that no one in the audience will respond by speaking *lashon hara* – for example, if no one knows the subject — one may praise him in public, but not excessively.
   c. If a person is known for his righteousness, one may praise him even before his enemies, because even if they speak *lashon hara* of him, no one will believe them.

 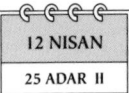 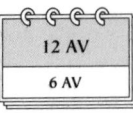

| 12 KISLEV | 12 NISAN | 12 AV | Daily Calendar |
| 16 KISLEV | 25 ADAR II | 6 AV | Leap Year |

3. More instances of *avak lashon hara*

a. It is forbidden to praise someone in a way that may cause him a loss. For example, one may not publicize someone's generosity, since dishonest borrowers may then approach him, and he will be hard-pressed to refuse them.

b. If something sounds like *lashon hara* but is not, it is forbidden due to *avak lashon hara*.

4. Dissociating from speakers of *lashon hara*

a. It is forbidden to live among neighbors who speak *lashon hara*. One must certainly not sit among them to hear their *lashon hara*, even if he does not believe it.

b. In the shul or Beis Midrash, one should not sit near people who speak *lashon hara*. Otherwise, they will influence him to join their gossip. They will also prevent him from responding to *Kaddish* and *Barechu* and hearing the Torah reading and the *chazan*'s repetition, in addition to the terrible sin of disrespecting a holy place by listening to *lashon hara* therein.

c. During one's set time for Torah study, he must be especially careful to avoid speakers of *lashon hara*. Otherwise, he will lose precious time from his studies. In the time that remains he will see no success, since he will be interrupted by constant banter. In addition to the sin of *lashon hara*, he will be punished for interrupting his Torah study.

d. If one's student regularly speaks *lashon hara*, and admonishing him would be ineffective, one must sever relations with him.

(continued on next page)

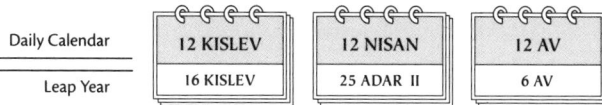

(continued from previous page)

e. If one finds himself trapped among a group of people speaking *lashon hara*, the proper response depends on the situation:
   i. If admonishing them may be beneficial, he must do so.
   ii. Even if admonishing them will not prevent them from speaking *lashon hara*, but it will not make matters worse, he must object.
   iii. If admonishing them will only increase their *lashon hara*, one should not object.
   iv. If one cannot admonish them but can change the subject, he must do so.

> ### ⁘ Pearls of Life ⁘
>
> With the faculty of hearing one can amass dozens of mitzvos each day, by answering Amen, *Kaddish*, *Barechu*, and *Kedushah*. So too, *chas v'shalom*, through the faculty of hearing one can cause terrible damage to his soul, by listening to *lashon hara* and the like.
>
> (*Shemiras HaLashon* II, ch. 30)

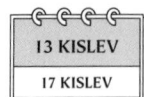 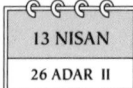 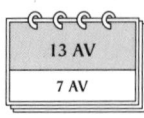

Daily Calendar

Leap Year

5. **Distancing one's children from *lashon hara***

   a. If one hears his children speaking *lashon hara*, he must chastise them and prevent them from speaking it.

   b. Parents must educate their children from a young age to refrain from *lashon hara* and other forbidden speech, such as controversy and lying.

   c. *Lashon hara* is so widespread because people grow up speaking as they wish, and no one objects. It is therefore very difficult for them to change. If children are trained from an early age not to speak *lashon hara*, curse, or lie, it will be easy for them to control their speech as they grow older. They will then merit great blessing in both this world and the next.

6. **Confidential information**

   It one has received information under the impression that it should remain confidential, or if it could cause the person who told him anguish or harm if revealed, then one may not reveal it without permission.

❖ *Pearls of Life* ❖

If a person accustoms himself to remain silent until it becomes second nature... he may rest assured that Hashem will protect him from speaking *lashon hara*.

(Shemiras HaLashon, Tevunah, ch. 1)

Daily Calendar	14 KISLEV	14 NISAN	14 AV
Leap Year	18 KISLEV	27 ADAR II	8 AV

KLAL 10:
Lashon Hara regarding Matters Bein Adam L'Chaveiro

1. **Correcting injustice**

   If a person witnesses an injustice involving theft, damage, humiliation, pain, or the like, and he knows for certain that the guilty party has not made amends, he may tell others in order to help the injured party or disgrace the guilty. However, the following conditions must be fulfilled.

2. **Conditions that must be fulfilled**

   a. One must have personally seen the injustice. If he only heard about it from others, he may not publicize it until he has verified that it is true.

   b. One must be certain that the guilty party is in fact liable according to Torah law.

   c. One must first admonish the guilty party (in a pleasant way), since he might repent, thereby obviating the need for *lashon hara*.

   d. One may not exaggerate. In addition, if he knows any point in defense of the guilty party, he may not conceal it.

   e. One's sole intention must be to gain practical benefit. He may not act out of personal hatred or malicious enjoyment of the guilty party's humiliation.

   f. If the practical benefit can be gained any other way, one may not speak *lashon hara*.

   g. The *lashon hara* may not cause the guilty party more harm than he would have received in Beis Din.

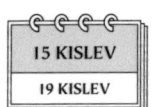 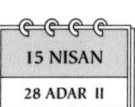 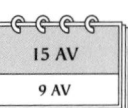

Daily Calendar	
Leap Year	

In a non leap-year the entire page is learned.

3. An additional condition

In order to speak against the guilty, one must be innocent of their crime. Otherwise, his intention in speaking against them is surely not noble.

In a leap year the following is learned on
20 Kislev, 29 Adar II, and 10 Av.

4. Intention to gain practical benefit (the fifth condition)

a. If the people he tells could help the injured party, it is certainly proper to tell them.

b. Even if the damage will not be repaired, it is still considered a benefit to disgrace the wicked, thus deterring others from following their evil ways. Furthermore, when the guilty party hears his disgrace, he may be encouraged to repent.

c. If none of these benefits will result, it is forbidden to relate the guilty party's deeds. For example, if the listeners are themselves wicked and will not disdain him for his crime, one may not tell them.

d. It is irrelevant whether the injured party has asked for assistance. When *lashon hara* is permitted, it is permitted even if he did not seek help; when it is forbidden, it is forbidden even if he did.

❧ *Pearls of Life* ❧

It is better to be thrown into a fiery furnace, than to publicly embarrass another person.

(*Berachos*, 43b)

| Daily Calendar | 16 KISLEV | 16 NISAN | 16 AV |
| Leap Year | 21 KISLEV | 1 NISAN | 11 AV |

5-6. Publicly disgracing speakers of *lashon hara*

a. It is permitted to publicly disgrace a speaker of *lashon hara*, provided that all the conditions discussed in rules 2-4 are fulfilled. One must also ascertain that the subject of the *lashon hara* has already heard of it. (Otherwise it is considered *rechilus* to cause the subject to hear of the injustice done to him.)

b. One may not tell someone that *lashon hara* was spoken against him, even if one's intention is to see justice done, and even if the injured party is his father or rabbi. This is considered *rechilus*.

c. If substantial benefit can be gained, one may publicly disgrace the speaker of *lashon hara* even if the subject has not heard of it (provided that the conditions discussed in rules 2-4 are fulfilled). For example, if the speaker is prone to continue spreading his tale, and his listeners will likely believe it, one may warn them that the speaker is a wicked person who unjustly demeans others and should be ignored.

❧ Pearls of Life ❧

Our Sages tell us that one must "make himself as if he was mute" (*Chullin* 89a). He should remember that for his many sins of improper speech he deserves to be made mute, yet Hashem has mercifully spared him. Realizing this, he should be careful never again to misuse his faculty of speech.

(*Shemiras HaLashon, Tevunah*, ch. 1)

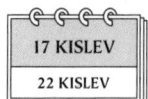 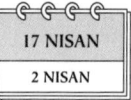 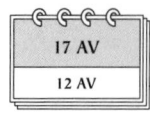

Daily Calendar

Leap Year

7–8. Admonishing the wicked

a. In rule 2, we stated that one must first admonish a wicked person, before speaking openly against him. However, if one realizes that the wicked person will ignore his admonishment, he may forgo this condition. In such a case one may only speak against him in the presence of three or more people (since it is forbidden to speak secretly against him, lest one appear as a liar).

b. If one fear's the wicked person's vengeance, he may speak secretly against him.

c. Upon hearing a person accused of evil deeds, one may not believe this to be true. He may only investigate the matter, and rebuke the subject if it is proven true.

❧ *Pearls of Life* ❧

All the pleasures of the World to Come await a person who controls his mouth and his desires. Self-control is worth more than any amount of fasting and self-affliction.

(Iggeres HaGra)

9. **Degrading the wicked before a private audience**

   If the speaker's audience knows that he is unafraid to speak in the presence of the wicked, and he is known never to lie, he may speak against the wicked, even to fewer than three people. (However, the other conditions listed in the beginning of this chapter must still be fulfilled).

10. ***Lashon hara* about matters *bein adam l'Makom***

    The rules outlined in this chapter also apply to sins *bein adam l'Makom* (between man and God). However, one may speak of such a sinner only if he sees him repeatedly and intentionally commit sins known to be forbidden (as discussed in Klal 4, rule 7).

⁂ *Pearls of Life* ⁂

Rabban Shimon ben Gamliel said, "All my days I was raised among the Sages, and I found nothing better than silence" (*Avos* 1:17). Having been raised among the Sages, he learned all their admirable, pious traits, and among them all he found no trait better than silence.

(*Shemiras HaLashon, Tevunah,* ch. 2)

 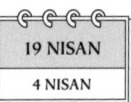 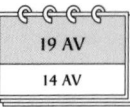

| 19 KISLEV | 19 NISAN | 19 AV | Daily Calendar |
| 24 KISLEV | 4 NISAN | 14 AV | Leap Year |

11. Speaking against those who have harmed us

a. If one has suffered theft, pain, or embarrassment through his dealings with someone, he may not publicize his grievances, even if he does not lie or exaggerate (see rule 13).

b. Upon hearing someone complain about the harm or embarrassment he suffered, one should ask exactly how the incident occurred. Even if the speaker would never lie, he may have omitted crucial details.

12. Speaking against those who have refused us favors

a. If one was refused a favor that rightly should have been granted, such as a loan, charity, or hospitality, he may not speak against those who refused him. In addition to *lashon hara*, this also transgresses, "Do not take vengeance and do not bear a grudge" (*Vayikra* 19:18).

b. One may certainly not speak against an entire community for not welcoming him properly, unless he tells someone who can rebuke them.

❧ *Pearls of Life* ❧

One who does not guard his mouth is not a man. He is no better than a speechless animal.

(Kavod Shamayim, ch. 2)

Daily Calendar	20 KISLEV	20 NISAN	20 AV
Leap Year	25 KISLEV	5 NISAN	15 AV

In a non leap-year the entire page is learned.

13-14. Enlisting help

a. If one has suffered theft or monetary damage, he may enlist help to regain what he is owed. For example, he may ask people to rebuke the thief, who might then return the money.

b. If practical benefit can be gained in non-monetary areas, it is also permitted to enlist help. For example, if one knows someone is planning to hurt or embarrass him, he may ask people to help prevent it.

In a leap year the following is learned on 26 Kislev, 6 Nisan, and 16 Av.

c. When seeking such help, one must be extremely careful to fulfill all the conditions listed in rule 2. Otherwise, he can easily stumble into the snare of speaking *lashon hara*.

❧ *Pearls of Life* ❧

"Death and life are in the hand of the tongue" (*Yalkut Shimoni* 34:721). The tongue is mightier than the sword. Through one's speech, he can condemn to death a person far away.

(*Shemiras HaLashon, Tevunah*, ch. 2)

The Laws of Lashon Hara: Klal 10

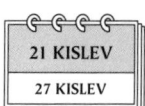 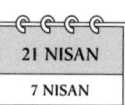 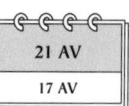

| 21 KISLEV | 21 NISAN | 21 AV | Daily Calendar |
| 27 KISLEV | 7 NISAN | 17 AV | Leap Year |

15. Preparing one's complaint

Before revealing one's grievances, he must consider exactly what to say and how to say it, in accordance with the conditions listed above. Otherwise, as he relates the story, his anger will overcome him, and he will most definitely violate the laws of *lashon hara*.

16. Defaming one who has defamed us

Reuven may not speak *lashon hara* against Shimon with the excuse that Shimon spoke against him first. There are two errors in this excuse.

a. Reuven may not believe that Shimon spoke *lashon hara* of him.

b. Reuven's intent is clearly not for the sake of Heaven but only to avenge himself against Shimon.

❧ *Pearls of Life* ❧

Speaking *lashon hara* is likened to denying Hashem's existence. Speaking *lashon hara* causes Hashem's Presence to forsake us. The sin of *lashon hara* reaches up to the Heavens. The sin of *lashon hara* kills three: the speaker, the listener, and the subject.

(*Kavod Shamayim*, ch. 2)

17. Avoiding blame

a. The required response

  i. If an offensive deed was performed, and one is asked who did it, even if he realizes that he is suspected, he may not reveal who really did it, even if he saw it done. He may only answer, "I did not do it."

  ii. If the guilty party will then be discovered by process of elimination, one may still plead innocent, provided that the deed was in fact forbidden. However, if the deed was not actually forbidden, but the person asking considered it improper, it is unclear whether one may plead innocent at his fellow's expense.

b. The admirable response
A pious person should go beyond the requirement of the law. Even if the deed was forbidden, he should not plead innocent and thereby cause the guilty party to be discovered and embarrassed. We find in the Gemara (*Sanhedrin* 11a) that even when they were not suspected, the Sages would accept responsibility for others' misdeeds in order to spare them embarrassment.

⁘ *Pearls of Life* ⁘

Not only did Yosef refrain from punishing his brothers for the harm they caused him, he dealt with them kindly in their time of need. This is the way of the righteous, and for this Hashem shows them mercy in this world and the next.

(*Zohar, Mikeitz*)

The Laws of Lashon Hara: Klal 10

 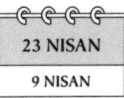 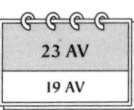

| 23 KISLEV | 23 NISAN | 23 AV | Daily Calendar |
| 29 KISLEV | 9 NISAN | 19 AV | Leap Year |

The Laws of *Rechilus*

KLAL 1:
The Prohibition Against Speaking Rechilus

1. **Speaking *rechilus***

   By speaking *rechilus*, one transgresses the prohibition "Do not go as a talebearer among your nation" (*Vayikra* 19:16). This terrible sin can lead to much bloodshed. Therefore, the verse continues, "Do not stand by the blood of your fellow." By speaking *rechilus*, one also transgresses numerous other prohibitions, as detailed in the introduction.

2. **The definition of *rechilus***

   Rechilus means telling Reuven what Shimon did or said against him. Even if according to the *rechilus* Shimon did nothing immoral or forbidden, and Shimon would not deny having done it, it is still considered *rechilus*, if it causes animosity between Reuven and Shimon.

In a non leap-year, the following page should also be learned.

| Daily Calendar | 23 KISLEV | 23 NISAN | 23 AV |
| Leap Year | 30 KISLEV | 10 NISAN | 20 AV |

In a non leap-year, this page is learned in addition to the previous one.

3. Rechilus without malicious intent

a. *Rechilus* is forbidden even if the speaker does not intend to provoke controversy, and even if he feels the subject acted correctly.

b. For example: If Reuven rebukes Shimon for something Shimon did against him, Shimon may not defend himself by saying that Levi did the same, if this defense will turn Reuven against Levi too.

❧ *Pearls of Life* ❧

When the wicked speak *lashon hara*, their words ascend before the Heavenly Throne of Glory. Angels descend from before Hashem to claim the souls of the wicked, and throw them into the depths of Gehinnom. Gehinnom then protests before Hashem, saying: 'Master of the Universe! I am unable to repay them the punishment they deserve. In the entire world, there is no fitting punishment. A speaker of *lashon hara* sins from the earth up unto the Heavens. Therefore, first shoot Your arrows from above, and then I will set upon him burning coals from below.

(*Tanna D'Vei Eliyahu*, ch. 18, cited in *Kavod Shamayim*)

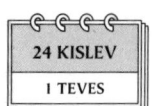  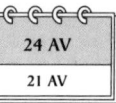

| 24 KISLEV | 24 NISAN | 24 AV | Daily Calendar |
| 1 TEVES | 11 NISAN | 21 AV | Leap Year |

4. Truthful *rechilus* and *rechilus* among enemies

Rechilus is forbidden even if it is entirely true, and even if the listener and the subject are already bitter enemies.

5. *Rechilus* under pressure

a. *Rechilus* is forbidden whether one is pressured into speaking it, or he speaks of his own volition. Even if one's father or rabbi pressures him to speak *rechilus*, he must not concede.

b. Even if one is pressured to speak *avak rechilus* (see below), he must not concede.

❦ *Pearls of Life* ❦

Rav Rafael of Hamburg, zt"l, would ask his guests not to speak about others in his home.

(Shemiras HaLashon, Tevunah, ch. 3)

❦ ❦ ❦

One must be very careful never to stand among a group of people, unless he is positive that they will not engage in forbidden speech.

(Shemiras HaLashon, Tevunah, ch. 3)

Daily Calendar	25 KISLEV	25 NISAN	25 AV
Leap Year	2 TEVES	12 NISAN	22 AV

6. *Rechilus* to prevent financial loss

a. *Rechilus* is forbidden even if one stands to suffer significant financial loss. For example, if one is suspected of a misdeed and stands to lose his job unless he reveals the true culprit, he still may not speak *rechilus* — even if he will then be unable to support his family.

b. However, *rechilus* is permitted in order to prevent harm or resolve a controversy, as discussed below in Klal 9.

7. *Rechilus* to prevent embarrassment

If one only stands to suffer ridicule and verbal abuse, it is certainly forbidden to speak *rechilus*. In such a situation, one should take comfort in the knowledge that for remaining silent in the face of humiliation, and suffering for the sake of a mitzvah, he is beloved to Hashem, and his face is destined to shine like the sun.

❖ *Pearls of Life* ❖

Our Sages tell us (*Shabbos* 88b): "Those who are insulted but do not insult back, hear their disgrace but do not respond, serve Hashem with love, and accept suffering with joy — of them the verse states, 'His beloved will be like the sun that goes forth in its might' (*Shoftim* 5:31)."

The commentaries explain that three levels are discussed here: (a) One who does not insult those who insult him, but he does respond; (b) he restrains himself from even responding, lest he be further insulted; (c) he restrains from responding out of love of Hashem, and accepts the suffering of insult with joy.

(*Shemiras HaLashon, Tevunah,* ch. 8)

 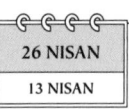 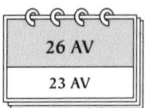

| 26 KISLEV | 26 NISAN | 26 AV | Daily Calendar |
| 3 TEVES | 13 NISAN | 23 AV | Leap Year |

8. **Responding to inquiries**

   a. Upon being asked, "What did he say about me?" if one can answer without lying or speaking *rechilus*, he must do so.

   b. If he cannot, he may lie to promote peace. However, he may not swear falsely.

9. **Hinting at *rechilus***

   a. *Rechilus* is forbidden even if one does not reveal the name of the subject, but through his story the subject can be identified.

   b. Even if the listener knows he was harmed or spoken against but does not know by whom, it is forbidden to hint at the identity of the culprit.

❖ *Pearls of Life* ❖

Silence is a trait beneficial to the wise; all the more so to the fool (*Pesachim* 99a). It is a protective fence around wisdom (*Avos* 3:13). When sitting among friends, it is better to be told, "Speak! Why are you silent?" rather than, "Silence! We cannot stand your banter."

(*Shemiras HaLashon, Tevunah*, ch. 2)

Daily Calendar	27 KISLEV	27 NISAN	27 AV
Leap Year	4 TEVES	14 NISAN	24 AV

10. Underhanded *rechilus*

It is forbidden to speak *rechilus* in an underhanded manner, as if one does not intend to provoke anger. For example, one may not remind a person of harm or embarrassment he once suffered, pretending not to know who caused it, and thereby remind the listener of his grudge.

11. *Rechilus* in writing; *rechilus* about merchandise

a. *Rechilus* is forbidden in writing, just as it is forbidden in speech.

b. It is forbidden to tell a merchant that someone slandered his merchandise.

❧ *Pearls of Life* ❧

When we judge others favorably, Hashem also judges us favorably (*Shabbos* 127b). The Gemara tells us that we must judge people favorably, even if they seem most likely to be guilty (ibid.).

(*Shemiras HaLashon, Tevunah*, ch. 4)

When we speak *lashon hara* against others, the accusing angels speak against us in the Heavenly Court.

(*Shemiras HaLashon* II, ch. 4)

The Laws of Rechilus: Klal 1

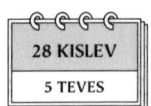 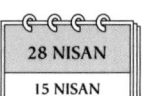 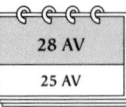

| 28 KISLEV | 28 NISAN | 28 AV | Daily Calendar |
| 5 TEVES | 15 NISAN | 25 AV | Leap Year |

KLAL 2:
Public Rechilus

1. **Public *rechilus***
   It is forbidden to speak *rechilus* in the presence of even one person, and it is certainly forbidden in the presence of many.

2. **Avak rechilus**
   a. It is forbidden to speak indirect *rechilus* (*avak rechilus*), as discussed below in Klal 8. Even if the comment could be interpreted positively, if one says it with negative intonations, it is forbidden.
   b. Even if one says it with positive intonations, but he is speaking to someone who always judges unfavorably or to a person who is already somewhat angry at the subject, it is forbidden.

❖ Pearls of Life ❖

The Midrash says that if a person habitually judges others negatively and speaks against them, the angels above also speak against him.

(*Shemiras HaLashon, Tevunah*, ch. 4)

Our Sages tell us that the world depends on the merit of those who remain silent amid controversy (*Chullin* 89a).

(*Shemiras HaLashon,, Tevunah*, ch. 11)

Daily Calendar	29 KISLEV	29 NISAN	29 AV
Leap Year	6 TEVES	16 NISAN	26 AV

3. *Rechilus* that is public knowledge

Even if Reuven spoke against Shimon in public, and therefore Shimon will likely hear of it from someone else, it is still forbidden to tell him.

It is forbidden even to tell a third party, since the information will eventually get back to Shimon.

4. Examples of *rechilus*

a. If a businessman considered leaving his partner in order to enter into a partnership with someone else, and then his plan failed and he decided to remain, it is forbidden to tell the first partner, even if the information has already been revealed to three people.

b. Similarly, if a *chasan* considered breaking his engagement and then reconsidered, it is forbidden to tell the *kallah* or her family.

c. If a rabbi of a shul considered moving to another shul and then reconsidered, it is forbidden to tell his congregants. In these and similar cases, although the subject may have done nothing wrong, the listeners might still be offended. Therefore it is *rechilus*.

❖ Pearls of Life ❖

If a person truly loves his fellow, he will never speak *lashon hara* against him and will always try to judge him as favorably as he can.

(*Shemiras HaLashon, Tevunah*, ch. 5)

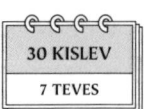 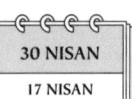 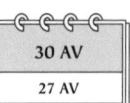

| 30 KISLEV | 30 NISAN | 30 AV | Daily Calendar |
| 7 TEVES | 17 NISAN | 27 AV | Leap Year |

KLAL 3:
Rechilus in the Subject's Presence or Absence

1. In the subject's presence

a. *Rechilus* is forbidden even if it is perfectly true, and even if the speaker would be willing to say it in the subject's presence. (For example, Reuven may not tell Shimon what Levi said against him, even if Reuven would be willing to tell him in Levi's presence.)

b. It is an even worse sin to accuse Levi in Shimon's presence, since Shimon will be more likely to believe it. Furthermore, one thereby causes Levi embarrassment, which the Torah forbids (as discussed in the introduction, prohibition no. 14).

❖ *Pearls of Life* ❖

All the Torah and mitzvos a person has amassed cannot counter one negative word that has left his mouth.

(Iggeres HaGra)

❖   ❖   ❖

If a person speaks badly about others and disgraces them, he will be spoken against and disgraced in return (in addition to his punishment in the World to Come).

(Shemiras HaLashon, Zechirah, ch. 11)

2. Confronting one's accusers

a. If Reuven speaks to Shimon against Levi, Reuven commits *lashon hara*. If Shimon then tells Levi what Reuven said, Shimon commits *rechilus*. If Levi then tells Reuven, "Shimon told me what you said about me," Levi also commits *rechilus*.

b. Even if Levi just tells Reuven, "I heard what you said about me," if Reuven will realize who told him, Levi has spoken *rechilus*.

3. Speaking *rechilus* to people other than the victim

a. It is forbidden to tell a third party what Reuven did to Shimon, since Shimon might find out, retroactively rendering the comment *rechilus*. Even if one warns the third party not to tell anyone, it is still forbidden, since the story will most likely include *lashon hara* about Reuven or Shimon.

b. It is certainly forbidden to tell Reuven what Shimon did against Reuven's relatives or friends, since Reuven will take offense.

4. Constructive *rechilus*

One may tell Reuven what Shimon did against Levi, in order that Reuven will rebuke Shimon. (See "The Laws of *Lashon Hara*," Klal 10, rules 5 and 6.)

❧ *Pearls of Life* ❧

When people speak recklessly and sully their mouths with *lashon hara*, one might regard them as utterly wicked and himself as perfectly righteous, since he guards his tongue. However, the Torah commands us to judge people favorably. Perhaps they do not know what is considered *lashon hara*, or they don't realize the severity of the prohibition.

(*Shemiras HaLashon, Tevunah*, ch. 1)

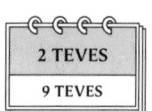	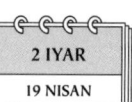	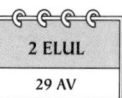	Daily Calendar
2 TEVES / 9 TEVES	2 IYAR / 19 NISAN	2 ELUL / 29 AV	Leap Year

KLAL 4:
Rechilus Known to the Subject

1. **Previously known *rechilus***

    Even if someone already knows what was done, it is forbidden to point out the injustice in it, thereby arousing his anger. For example, if a person lost a case in Beis Din, one may not tell him that he was misjudged.

2. **Repeating *rechilus***

    If Reuven defamed Shimon in the presence of Levi and Yehuda, even if Levi has already told Shimon, Yehuda may not also tell him.

3. **Atoning for *rechilus***

    To atone for speaking *rechilus*, one must appease the person he spoke against and ask his forgiveness. One must then repent before Hashem for committing this sin. This process is discussed above ("The Laws of *Lashon Hara*," end of Klal 4).

> ### ❧ *Pearls of Life* ❧
>
> The sin of *lashon hara* reaches up to the Heavens.... It is a terribly severe sin, since it incites Hashem's anger upon the world.
>
> (*Kavod Shamayim*, ch. 2)

KLAL 5:
Listening to and Accepting Rechilus

1. **Accepting *rechilus***
   a. It is forbidden by Torah law to believe *rechilus*. By doing so, one transgresses several positive and prohibitive commandments. Accepting *rechilus* is even worse than speaking it.
   b. Our Sages tell us that *lashon hara* and *rechilus* can kill the one who spoke it, the one who accepted it, and the one of whom it was spoken. A person who speaks or accepts *lashon hara* is fit to be thrown to the dogs.

2. **Listening to *rechilus***
   a. Just listening to *rechilus* is forbidden, even if one has not yet decided to believe it.
   b. If there is practical benefit to be gained from the *rechilus*, it is permitted to listen. For example, if one is told that someone plans to harm him or his possessions, he may listen to the story in order to protect himself. However, he may not believe for certain that it is true.
   c. The proper response upon hearing *rechilus* is identical to the proper response to *lashon hara*, as detailed above in Klal 6.

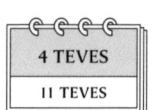 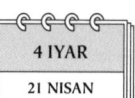 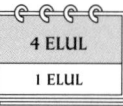

| 4 TEVES | 4 IYAR | 4 ELUL | Daily Calendar |
| 11 TEVES | 21 NISAN | 1 ELUL | Leap Year |

3. **Investigating threats**

   a. If one has reason to suspect that someone plans to harm him or his possessions, he may ask around if this is true, in order to protect himself. He need not fear that he will be told *lashon hara* or *rechilus*.

   b. Even if one has seen only slightly suspicious behavior from the subject, he may still investigate to determine the reason for this behavior. However, he may rely on the information he receives only in order to protect himself. He may not believe for certain that it is true.

   c. Even if one has only heard from others that someone wants to harm him, but he has seen no evidence to support this, he may still investigate further to protect himself.

4. **Suspecting *rechilus* to be true**

   The general rule is that one may suspect *rechilus* to be true, only in as far as it is necessary to protect himself from harm. Regarding no other matter may he even suspect it to be true. Therefore, the following conditions apply:

   a. Although one may do his utmost to protect himself, in his heart he must not entertain any doubt at all that the suspect is completely innocent.

   b. It is forbidden to harm the suspect in any way, by causing him monetary loss, embarrassment, or the like.

   c. It is forbidden by Torah law to hate the suspect, even if one does not act on this hatred.

   d. It is forbidden to refuse any monetary obligations he has toward the suspect.

   e. One is obligated to fulfill toward the suspect all the mitzvos of charity and kindness required by the Torah.

Daily Calendar	5 TEVES	5 IYAR	5 ELUL
Leap Year	12 TEVES	22 NISAN	2 ELUL

5. **Investigating what was said against us**

   a. Some people have the bad habit of inquiring as to what was said about them, even if there is no practical benefit to knowing. They pressure others into revealing insults supposedly said behind their backs, believe them with utter certainty, and thus become bitter enemies of those who purportedly insulted them.

   b. This practice violates several prohibitions. It is forbidden even to listen to *rechilus*, let alone pressure others into speaking it. In addition to one's own sin of listening to *rechilus*, he is also accountable for causing others to sin by speaking it.

   c. Therefore one must refrain from investigating what was said or done against him, unless there is practical benefit to be had, such as guarding himself from potential harm.

⁘ *Pearls of Life* ⁘

The Holy One Blessed Be He says to the Jewish people: "My beloved children, do I lack anything that I need to ask it of you? What do I ask of you? Only that you love one another, honor one another, and revere one another."

(*Tanna D'Vei Eliyahu*, ch. 28)

Controversy is so destructive that it can endanger lives and even cause death.

(*Shemiras HaLashon, Zechirah*, ch. 15)

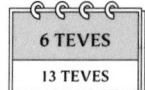 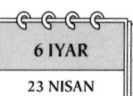 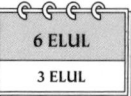

Daily Calendar

Leap Year

6. **Accepting another's negative opinion**

    Even if one already knows the facts of the situation, it is forbidden to accept another person's negative interpretation of them. For example, if Reuven harmed Shimon, Shimon must judge him favorably. If Levi convinces Shimon not to judge Reuven favorably, Levi has spoken *rechilus*.

7. **Atonement for accepting *rechilus***

    If a person accepted *rechilus*, his atonement depends on three factors:

    a. He must force himself to no longer believe it. (Even if he cannot believe that he was told an outright lie, perhaps a significant detail was added or omitted, or he was presented with a slightly warped version of the story.)

    b. He must resolve to never again accept *lashon hara* or *rechilus*.

    c. He must confess before Hashem his sin of accepting *rechilus*.

    If he spread the *rechilus*, his atonement depends on the factors discussed above in "The Laws of *Lashon Hara*," Klal 6, rule 12.

❧ *Pearls of Life* ❧

If a person were to accidentally eat *treif* meat, how heartbroken would he be? He would remember this sin for the rest of his life. Yet people speak *lashon hara* and instigate disputes. Even if they later realize their sin, they do not take it to heart quite so much, and search for ways to prevent this from happening again. This is a clear proof the yetzer hara has blinded us to the terrible sin of *lashon hara*, which is a Torah prohibition just like eating *treif*.

(*Shemiras HaLashon* II, ch. 7).

| Daily Calendar | 7 TEVES | 7 IYAR | 7 ELUL |
| Leap Year | 14 TEVES | 24 NISAN | 4 AV |

KLAL 6:
Additional Rules of Rechilus

1. **Rechilus spoken in public**
   a. Even if *rechilus* was spoken in public, this is no proof that it is true. Therefore, one may not believe it.
   b. However, if the *rechilus* is of practical relevance, one may suspect it might be true in order to protect himself. If it is not of practical relevance, one may not investigate the matter further, by asking others, "What did he say about me?"

2. **Rechilus in the subject's presence**
   Even if *rechilus* is spoken in the subject's presence, it is forbidden to accept it. For example, if Reuven tells Shimon what Levi said or did against him, and Levi is present but does not object, Shimon still may not believe it to be true. Even if Levi usually objects when he hears things he dislikes, and in this case he did not deny the accusation, this is still not considered a confession, and one may not believe it to be true.

❖ *Pearls of Life* ❖

The Zohar teaches that *lashon hara* arouses the Great Accuser, bringing death and destruction to the world.

(*Kavod Shamayim*, ch. 2)

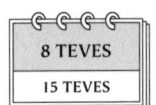 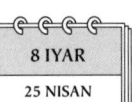 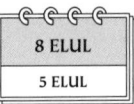

| Daily Calendar |
| Leap Year |

3. **Suspicions and accusations**

   a. If a person suffered a business loss, he may not baselessly suspect that another Jew caused it through slander or other foul means. For example, if a person was fired from his job, he may not baselessly suspect that a co-worker slandered him to his employer.

   b. Even if he heard that someone caused his loss, or if someone was accused and did not deny it, he may not believe it. One may only suspect that the matter may be true in order to protect himself.

4. ***Rechilus* heard from several people**

   Even if one heard the same *rechilus* from several people, or if rumor has it that someone spoke or did something against him, he may not believe it.

❧ *Pearls of Life* ❧

The Zohar states in the name of Rebbe Akiva that even if a person is the greatest tzaddik (righteous person) in the world, if he speaks wrongfully before Hashem, or speaks *lashon hara* against Jews — the worst punishment awaits him.

(Shemiras HaLashon, Tevunah, ch. 7)

Daily Calendar	9 TEVES	9 IYAR	9 ELUL
Leap Year	16 TEVES	26 NISAN	6 AV

In a non leap-year the entire page is learned.

5-7. Accepting *rechilus* from a person as trustworthy as two witnesses

a. It is forbidden to accept *rechilus* even from a person as trustworthy as two witnesses, and even if according to the story there is no way to judge the subject favorably.

b. If there is a practical benefit to knowing the *rechilus*, one may accept it from such a person. However, he may not reveal it to others, unless there is also a practical benefit in doing so.

In a leap year the following is learned on 17 Teves, 27 Nisan, and 7 Elul.

c. Today, nobody is considered as trustworthy as two witnesses. Therefore one may never believe *rechilus*, even if he heard it from his parents or his wife. He may only suspect it to be true in order to protect himself.

⁜ *Pearls of Life* ⁜

Every Jew must pray for mercy on behalf of Klal Yisrael and advocate for our nation before Hashem. Although our spiritual level has indeed deteriorated, there are still many people who learn Torah and observe mitzvos. There are many supporters of Torah, kind people, and patrons of charity in every community.

(*Shemiras HaLashon, Tevunah*, ch. 7)

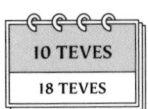 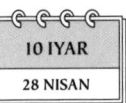 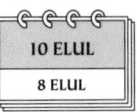

| Daily Calendar |
| Leap Year |

In a non leap-year the entire page is learned.

8. Accepting *rechilus* spoken innocently ('*masiach l'fi tumo*')

It is forbidden to accept *rechilus* even from a person who spoke without malicious intent and had no desire to stir controversy.

9. Accepting *rechilus* based on circumstantial evidence

If circumstantial evidence supports the *rechilus*, it may be believed, provided that five conditions are fulfilled:

a. There is no way to judge the subject favorably.
b. The evidence is conclusive.
c. One saw the evidence himself, and did not just hear about it from others.
d. There is practical benefit to knowing the *rechilus*.
e. Even if all these conditions are fulfilled, one may not spread the *rechilus*, unless there is practical benefit in doing so. One may certainly not rely on the *rechilus* to hurt the subject or cause him monetary loss.

In a leap year the following is learned on
19 Teves, 29 Nisan, and 9 Elul.

10. Repaying slander with slander

As an example of this last clause, if Reuven has conclusive evidence that Shimon caused him a business loss by slandering him, he may not slander Shimon in return.

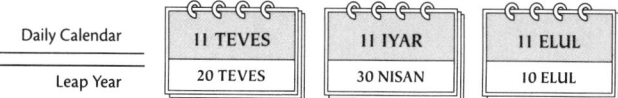

| Daily Calendar | 11 TEVES | 11 IYAR | 11 ELUL |
| Leap Year | 20 TEVES | 30 NISAN | 10 ELUL |

KLAL 7:
The Speaker and the Audience of Rechilus

1. The speaker and the subject

a. It is forbidden for any Jewish man or woman to speak *rechilus*.

b. It is forbidden to speak *rechilus* about any Jewish man or woman, whether adult or child, including one's relatives.

❖ *Pearls of Life* ❖

A person should train himself to serenely accept whatever happens to him. As our Sages say: "Train yourself to accept suffering and forgive insult" (*Avos d'Rabbi Nasan*). Thereby, he will find it much easier to guard his tongue.

(*Shemiras HaLashon, Tevunah*, ch. 8)

❖   ❖   ❖

If a person advocates before Hashem on behalf of the Jewish people, he becomes a vessel for the holy light of the "Chamber of Merit," where the righteousness of Israel is recalled.

(*Shemiras HaLashon, Tevuna* ch. 7)

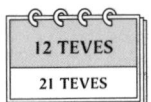 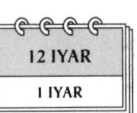 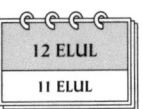

Daily Calendar

Leap Year

2. *Rechilus* against Torah scholars and ignoramuses

It is forbidden to speak *rechilus* even against an *am ha'aretz* (Torah ignoramus), but the punishment for speaking against a Torah scholar is much more severe.

✣ *Pearls of Life* ✣

Rebbe Beroka of Chozai was standing in the marketplace of Lefet, when Eliyahu HaNavi appeared to him.

"Is there anybody here who is a son of the World to Come?" he asked Eliyahu....

"Those people are sons of the World to Come," Eliyahu said. Rebbe Beroka then approached them and asked them what their special merit was.

"We are happy people, and we like to make others happy," they answered. "When we see someone depressed, we cheer him. When we see people quarrel, we help them resolve their differences."

(*Taanis* 22a)

3. **Telling *rechilus* to the subject's relatives**

   If Reuven spoke against Shimon, it is forbidden to tell Shimon's relatives — even if one warns them not to tell Shimon — since they too will be angry at Reuven. This is true even if he tells them no *lashon hara* against Reuven or Shimon.

4. **Telling *rechilus* to a Gentile**

   It is forbidden to tell a Gentile *rechilus* about a Jew. For example, one may not tell a Gentile that the merchandise a Jew sold him is faulty or that the Jew's labor was done poorly. Telling *rechilus* to a Gentile is a much greater sin than telling it to a Jew.

> ❧ *Pearls of Life* ❧
>
> "When I hear myself insulted in public, I imagine a pair of scales. On one side I imagine my sins; on the other side I imagine the insults. I then see that my sins are much heavier, and I remain silent, accepting my punishment as just. I do the same any time I suffer from the deeds or words of others."
>
> (*Sefer Chareidim*, cited in *Shemiras HaLashon*, *Tevunah*, ch. 8)

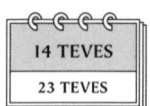 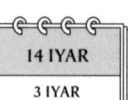 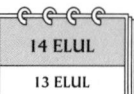

Daily Calendar	
Leap Year	

14 TEVES	14 IYAR	14 ELUL
23 TEVES	3 IYAR	13 ELUL

5. **Accepting *rechilus***

It is forbidden to accept *rechilus* from anyone, even from one's spouse. If one's wife tells him *rechilus*, he should strongly rebuke her, since her *rechilus* could bring him to anger and controversy.

> ❖ *Pearls of Life* ❖
>
> Once there was a gentile who came before Shammai and said, "Convert me to Judaism, on condition that you teach me the entire Torah while standing on one leg." Shammai took a measuring rod and chased him away.
>
> The gentile then came before Hillel with the same request. "What is hateful to you, don't do to others — this is the entire Torah, and the rest is just commentary. Now go and learn," was Hillel's response.
>
> (*Shabbos* 31a)

KLAL 8:
Avak Rechilus

1. **The prohibition against *avak rechilus***

   It is forbidden to say things that imply *rechilus* or will lead others to speak *rechilus*. This is called "*avak rechilus* — the dust of *rechilus*." For example, one may not tell Reuven that his name was mentioned to Shimon, and Shimon said, "Let's not speak of Reuven. I don't want to say what he did." Telling Reuven is likely to incite him against Shimon, since Shimon implied negative sentiments toward him. It is similarly forbidden to tell Reuven that Shimon made disparaging insinuations against him.

2. **Praising someone to those who will find fault**

   Avak rechilus also includes praising someone for something that will make others upset at him and thus perhaps cause him harm. For example, one may not praise a person to his spouse or business partner for his generosity, since they might consider the money unwisely spent, and be angry at him for his generosity.

3. **Not mentioning favors done for others**

   When refused a favor, one may not ask, "Why did you do the favor for Reuven, but not for me?" The benefactor might be upset at Reuven for publicizing the favor and thereby encouraging unwanted solicitors.

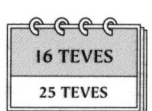 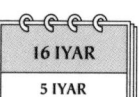 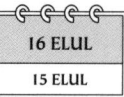

| 16 TEVES | 16 IYAR | 16 ELUL | Daily Calendar |
| 25 TEVES | 5 IYAR | 15 ELUL | Leap Year |

4. **Offensive *rechilus***

   a. It is forbidden to tell Reuven that Shimon said of him something that, although not really an insult, may cause offense. For example, telling Reuven that Shimon said he is old.

   b. It is forbidden to tell Reuven that Shimon even insinuated that he engages in improper conduct, even if the conduct is not forbidden. For example, telling Reuven that Shimon said he is always cooking (thus implying that he overeats).

5. **Keeping secrets**

   It is forbidden to reveal a secret, even if no *lashon hara* or *rechilus* is involved. (Revealing secrets is much more severe than speaking *avak rechilus*.)

❦ *Pearls of Life* ❦

Rav Huna son of Rebbe Yehoshua was deathly ill. Hashem decreed that since Rav Huna was accustomed to forgive offense, the Heavenly Court should not be too exacting with him. He then recovered from his illness.

(*Rosh Hashana* 17)

Daily Calendar	17 TEVES	17 IYAR	17 ELUL
Leap Year	26 TEVES	6 IYAR	16 ELUL

KLAL 9:
When Rechilus Is Permitted

1. **Preventing a harmful partnership**
   If someone is considering hiring an employee or taking on a partner who will certainly cause him harm, one is obligated to warn him, but only if the following five conditions have been fulfilled.

2. **Five conditions for the above ruling**
   a. The risk in question must constitute a real harm.
   b. One may not exaggerate the risk.
   c. One's intent must be to provide a practical benefit, and not be motivated by hatred for the subject. One must be reasonably certain that the person in danger will accept his warning. Otherwise, no benefit will result.
   d. There is no other way to prevent the danger.
   e. No harm will befall the subject, other than not receiving the job or partnership in question.

⁂ *Pearls of Life* ⁂

The armies of King David were perfectly righteous in all other matters, yet since they spoke *lashon hara* they suffered casualties in battle. The armies of King Ahab were wicked idolaters, yet since they did not speak *lashon hara*, they returned from battle unscathed.

(Talmud Yerushalmi, Pei'ah ch. 1)

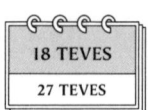 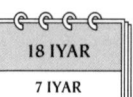 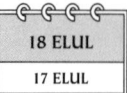

18 TEVES	Daily Calendar
27 TEVES	Leap Year
18 IYAR	
7 IYAR	
18 ELUL	
17 ELUL	

3–4. Protecting others from harm

a. If someone has threatened to hit, disgrace, or otherwise harm another, and he has done so on several previous occasions — or it is otherwise clear that his threat is not idle — one must warn the potential victim. However, the five conditions listed above must be fulfilled. In addition:

b. One may warn the potential victim only if he has already admonished the antagonist to no avail, or if he knows his admonishment would be fruitless.

c. One may warn the potential victim only if he foresees that the victim will do nothing more than protect himself. However, if the warning will incite him to harm his antagonist first, thus exacerbating the dispute, it is forbidden to warn him.

❖ *Pearls of Life* ❖

There is a great advantage to the Torah learned by a person who does not blemish his lips with *lashon hara*. This is as our Sages say regarding Torah learned by innocent school children, "We cannot compare words spoken by a mouth free of sin, to those spoken by a sinful mouth."

(Zechor L'Miriam, ch. 7)

5-6. After the partnership has been settled

Even after Reuven and Shimon have verbally agreed to form a partnership, Levi may still warn Reuven against it and dissuade him from finalizing the deal. Once the partnership is legally binding, however, Levi may not warn Reuven if this will cause him to terminate the deal or otherwise harm his partner, unless Levi first receives permission from Beis Din.

❦ *Pearls of Life* ❦

When a person stands in judgment, he is careful with every word he speaks, lest it be used against him. He knows that a single slip of the tongue may bring a guilty verdict upon him. Our Sages tell us that even the light conversation between husband and wife are brought before them in their hour of judgment (*Chagigah* 5b). We will be forced to give an accounting for every word we have spoken throughout our lives.

(*Zechor L'Miriam*, ch. 3).

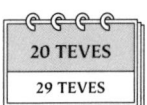 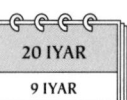 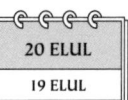

20 TEVES	20 IYAR	20 ELUL	Daily Calendar
29 TEVES	9 IYAR	19 ELUL	Leap Year

7. **Revealing damage that was done**

   When telling Reuven that Shimon robbed or otherwise harmed him, Levi must fulfill the five conditions outlined above. Levi must also first try to admonish Shimon. If this admonition fails, Levi may then inform Reuven.

8. ***Rechilus* under pressure**

   If the conditions outlined above are fulfilled, Levi must tell Reuven even if he is not asked to do so. If the conditions are not fulfilled, Levi may not tell Reuven, even if Reuven pressures him to do so.

9. **Telling *rechilus* to people other than the victim**

   It is also considered *rechilus* to tell people other than the victim (since he will eventually hear of it), unless the conditions outlined above are fulfilled (see Klal 3, rule 3).

❧ *Pearls of Life* ❧

One should accustom himself to always judge people favorably, in fulfillment of the verse: "With righteousness, you shall judge your fellow." The "interest" of the reward for doing so is enjoyed in this world, while the principal reward remains intact in the World to Come.

(*Shemiras HaLashon, Tevunah*, ch. 4)

10. Warning a purchaser about a dishonest vendor

If an unsuspecting shopper enters a store, and one knows the proprietor will try to cheat him by selling faulty merchandise, using dishonest weights or measures (even slightly), or overcharging (by at least one-sixth of the market value), one must warn the shopper not to buy there, even if he has already agreed to buy the merchandise (but has not yet bought it). However, the conditions outlined in rule 2 must be fulfilled.

> ### ❖ *Pearls of Life* ❖
>
> If peace reigns among Israel, and no one speaks evil of another, the Satan cannot speak against us before the Heavenly Court — even concerning idolatry, the most heinous of sins.
>
> (*Shemiras HaLashon, Zechirah,* ch. 2)
>
>
>
> Our Sages advise us to always hasten to greet others. Even if we know someone dislikes us, we should greet him warmly. This overture will cause him to love us. If his heart fails to soften, then in the merit of pursuing peace Hashem will subjugate our enemies before us.
>
> (*Shemiras HaLashon, Zechirah,* ch. 11)

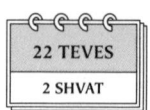 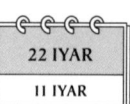 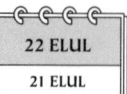

| 22 TEVES | 22 IYAR | 22 ELUL | Daily Calendar |
| 2 SHVAT | 11 IYAR | 21 ELUL | Leap Year |

11. **After the purchase**

    After the shopper has made a purchase, one may tell him he was cheated only if he is eligible for reimbursement according to Torah law. In such a case, one must fulfill the five conditions outlined below. If he is ineligible, one may not tell him he was cheated, even if he asks.

12. **Five conditions for the above ruling**

    a. One may not exaggerate the fraud.

    b. One's intention must be to pursue truth and help the cheated shopper, not to rejoice over the vendor's embarrassment. For this reason, one may tell the shopper only if he will likely seek a refund. Otherwise, it is forbidden to tell him, since no practical benefit will be achieved.

    c. If admonishing the vendor will cause him to return the money, one must do so rather than tell the shopper.

    d. If one can help the shopper regain his money without telling him that he was cheated, one must do so.

    e. One must warn the shopper not to tell the vendor who revealed the fraud, since this constitutes *rechilus*. If the shopper will not heed this warning, it is unclear whether one may tell him.

⁑ *Pearls of Life* ⁑

When we speak *lashon hara* about someone else, we take his sins upon ourselves and he takes our mitzvos.

(*Chovos HaLevavos* 7:9)

| Daily Calendar | 23 TEVES | 23 IYAR | 23 ELUL |
| Leap Year | 3 SHVAT | 12 IYAR | 22 ELUL |

13. If the shopper will take unjust measures

If the shopper will take unjust measures, then there are several other conditions which must be fulfilled in order that this not constitute *rechilus*. Even if all these conditions are fulfilled, it is still forbidden to tell him, since by doing so one incites him to commit a crime. Therefore, in such a case one may tell him only if Beis Din grants permission.

❧ *Pearls of Life* ❧

Rav Chama son of Rebbe Chanina asked: What is the recourse for a speaker of *lashon hara*? If he is a Torah scholar, let him toil in Torah. If he is ignorant of Torah, let him humble himself, as the verse says, "[A healing for the tongue, is the Tree of Life], and for those whose tongues slip, let their spirits be humbled."

Rebbe Acha son of Rebbe Chanina argued: If a person spoke *lashon hara*, he has no recourse, since it was revealed to David by *ru'ach hakodesh* (Divine inspiration) that he is cut off (*kareis*) from Hashem, as the verse says, "May Hashem cut off all slippery lips, all tongues that speak haughtily." Rather, what is the recourse to avoid speaking *lashon hara* in the first place? If he is a Torah scholar, let him toil in Torah. If he is ignorant of Torah, let him humble himself.

(*Arachin* 15b)

The Laws of Rechilus: Klal 9

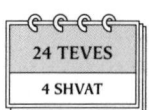 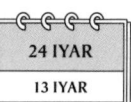 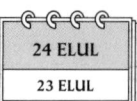

| 24 TEVES | 24 IYAR | 24 ELUL | Daily Calendar |
| 4 SHVAT | 13 IYAR | 23 ELUL | Leap Year |

14. Avoiding blame

a. If Reuven was harmed and asks who did it, even if one realizes he is suspected, he may not reveal the culprit, even if he witnessed the incident. He may only answer, "I did not do it."

b. If a committee made a private vote, and the majority ruled against Reuven, it is forbidden for any member of the committee to reveal to Reuven that he voted in Reuven's favor. Such disclosure is considered *rechilus* against the other members of the committee.

15. An example of *rechilus* in business dealings

a. Reuven wished to purchase merchandise but lacked money, so he asked the merchant to reserve the goods for him, and he would pay for them later. Before Reuven returned, however, Shimon pressured the merchant to sell the merchandise to him instead, and the merchant agreed. The merchant may not then tell Reuven, "Shimon pressured me into selling him your merchandise."

No practical benefit will be achieved by telling Reuven, since he cannot force Shimon to return the merchandise. Reuven will only be angry at Shimon. Therefore, telling Reuven constitutes *rechilus*.

b. If the merchant was not pressured to sell it to Shimon, but he blames Shimon nonetheless, this is "*motzi shem ra—* spreading a false rumor," which is much worse than truthful *rechilus*.

c. Even if the merchant does not blame Shimon but simply says he sold it to him by accident, Reuven may still be upset at Shimon. Therefore, such a statement is still considered *rechilus*. Instead, the merchant should just say he sold it without saying to whom.

Lashon Hara in Business

1. **Business partnerships, before they are made binding**

   a. If Reuven wishes to enter into a partnership with someone known to be untrustworthy, one must warn him before he settles the deal. However, all the conditions outlined above in Klal 9, rule 2, must be fulfilled.

   b. If Reuven wishes to enter into a partnership with Shimon, who is trustworthy but financially unstable, one may not warn him. Perhaps despite Shimon's previous financial troubles, this partnership will succeed.

   However, if Reuven explicitly states that he seeks only a financially stable partner, perhaps one may tell him, provided that Shimon's situation is truly severe. One must also ensure that Shimon will not discover that he advised against the partnership, since this discovery will cause arguments and hatred. In such a case, it is better to feign ignorance.

   c. If Shimon has already caused several people to lose money through similar partnerships, and Reuven inquires about Shimon, one should tell him the truth. If Reuven does not inquire, it is unclear whether one should tell him.

2. **Business partnerships, after they are made binding**

   a. Once Reuven has entered into a legally binding partnership with an untrustworthy partner, one may warn him only if he will do nothing more than protect himself. In such a case, one must abide by the conditions discussed in Klal 9, rule 2.

   b. If Reuven will annul the partnership or otherwise harm his partner without permission from Beis Din, one may not tell him.

   In a non leap-year, the following page should also be learned.

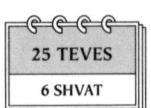 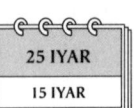 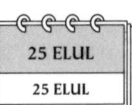

25 TEVES / 6 SHVAT	Daily Calendar
25 IYAR / 15 IYAR	
25 ELUL / 25 ELUL	Leap Year

In a non leap-year, this page is learned in addition to the previous one.

3. Not encouraging a detrimental partnership

It is forbidden to advise someone to enter into a possibly detrimental business partnership or *shidduch* that the adviser himself would avoid (due to the subject's untrustworthiness or financial instability).

❧ *Pearls of Life* ❧

When speaking *lashon hara*, one should not think that no one is present but himself and his audience. The Heavenly Court stands over him at that moment and records every word he speaks. As the Midrash says on the verse "Do not say before the angel that it was inadvertent. Why should Hashem be angered by your voice?" (*Koheles* 5:5). Do not say, "I will speak *lashon hara*, and no one will know." Hashem warns us, "Beware, I am sending an angel who will stand beside you and record everything you say about your fellow" (*Devarim Rabbah* 6:5).

At the time of one's judgment, all his words are brought before him, as our Sages say of the verse "He tells man all he has spoken" (*Amos* 4:13). Even light banter between man and wife is repeated before him at the time of his judgment (*Chagigah* 5b).

(*Kavod Shamayim*, ch. 1)

Daily Calendar	26 TEVES	26 IYAR	26 ELUL
Leap Year	7 SHVAT	16 IYAR	26 ELUL

Lashon Hara regarding Shidduchim

4. Revealing the faults of a *shidduch*

If someone is considering a marriage but is unaware of substantial faults in his prospective partner, and he would refuse the *shidduch* if he knew, one should tell him. However, the following conditions must be fulfilled.

5. Faults that may not be revealed

a. It is forbidden to reveal insubstantial faults. For example, some people consider it a fault to be overly innocent. They might not wish to marry a boy who does not make derisive jokes like other boys in his circles. Yet in truth this is not a fault at all. Therefore it may not be revealed.

b. It is forbidden to reveal embarrassing incidents in the history of the family. Since they have no bearing on the present, revealing them is considered *lashon hara*.

❖ *Pearls of Life* ❖

If one sits among people who speak *lashon hara* or profanity, or mock Torah and mitzvos, but he does not object, although he knows for certain that they would not listen to him, he will still be punished. They might misinterpret his silence as agreement with their evil words.

(*Chovas HaShemirah*, ch. 14)

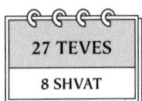 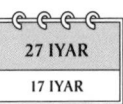 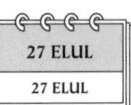

| 27 TEVES | 27 IYAR | 27 ELUL | Daily Calendar |
| 8 SHVAT | 17 IYAR | 27 ELUL | Leap Year |

6–7. Faults that may be revealed

a. If a prospective marriage partner has a medical condition unknown to the other, one may tell the latter even if he does not ask, provided that the following conditions are fulfilled.

　　i. One must be certain that this is indeed an illness, not just a general weakness.

　　ii. One may not exaggerate the condition.

　　iii. One's intention must be for practical benefit, not out of hatred.

　　iv. A practical benefit will be gained. If the listener would marry this person nonetheless, one may not tell him.

b. If one prospective partner is known to be an *apikores*, even slightly, one must reveal it to the other. In this case, one need not fulfill the conditions stated above. However, if one only heard of the *apikorsus* but does not know for certain that it exists, he must tell the other prospective partner that this is an unverified concern.

c. One may not tell the girl's parents that the boy has little Torah knowledge, since they could have tested him had they wished.

d. If the prospective bride's family is known for immoral conduct, one must tell the groom. Only the fourth condition — practical benefit –must be fulfilled in order to tell him.

8. **Revealing deceit before the engagement**

   If the parents of one side do not intend to deliver the dowry they promise, one may tell the other side before the engagement is finalized, if the following conditions are fulfilled:

   a. One must be certain of their intent to deceive.

   b. A practical benefit must be gained. If the other side would be willing to make the match even without the dowry, one may not tell them, unless doing so would help them receive the money that was promised.

   c. If both sides deceive each other, one may not tell either of them.

   In addition to these conditions, one must fulfill those discussed above in Klal 9, rule 2. Therefore, one must not be hasty to reveal such information.

9. **Revealing deceit after the engagement**

   a. If the engagement has already been finalized, then one may reveal the deceit only if the other side will merely take precautions and seek advice to avoid being cheated, doing no more than authorized by Beis Din. The conditions listed above must also be fulfilled.

   b. If the other side will rely on the information to break the engagement without authorization of Beis Din, one may not reveal the deceit.

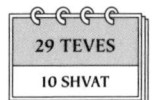 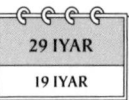 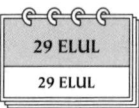

Daily Calendar

Leap Year

10. Revealing illness after the engagement

a. If the prospective partner has a medical condition unknown to the other side, one may tell that side even after the engagement has been finalized. However, one must fulfill the conditions listed above in Klal 9, rule 2.

b. If one has no personal knowledge of the illness, having only heard of it from others, he may not tell the other side, even with the disclaimer that he only heard it, and it might not be true. However, if the other side will not believe it for certain and will only investigate the matter, one may tell that side, provided that the conditions listed above are fulfilled.

11. Revealing immoral conduct or *apikorsus* after the engagement

a. If the prospective partner's family is known for immoral conduct, one must tell the other side, even if it will break the engagement. All the more so if the prospective partner is an *apikores*. The conditions listed above need not be fulfilled in either of these cases.

b. If one has no personal knowledge of these issues, having only heard of them from others, he must still inform the other side. However, he must tell them that he is only conveying hearsay which they should not believe until they investigate it further.

SUMMARY

A person must take heed in all his deeds, and especially in his speech, not to interfere with the affairs of others, unless: (a) he is well aware of every relevant detail; (b) his intention is for practical benefit, not out of hatred; (c) nothing contrary to Torah or Rabbinic law will result from his involvement. Then Hashem will help him not to fall into the trap of *lashon hara*.

Index

❖ Introduction to the Laws of *Lashon Hara* and *Rechilus*

THE SEVENTEEN PROHIBITIONS OF *LASHON HARA*

1. "Do not go as a talebearer amongst your nation" (*Vayikra* 19:16). 32
2. "Do not bear false testimony" (*Shemos* 23:1). 32
3. "Guard yourself from the plague of *tzaraas* by being exceedingly careful and diligent" (*Devarim* 24:8). 33
4. "Do not place a stumbling block before the blind" (*Vayikra* 19:14). 33
5. "Guard yourself, lest you forget Hashem, your God" (*Devarim* 8:11). 34
6. "Do not desecrate My holy Name" (*Vayikra* 22:32). 34
7. "Do not hate your brother in your heart" (*Vayikra* 19:17). 35
8–9. "Do not take vengeance, and do not bear a grudge" (*Vayikra* 19:18). 35
10. "A single witness may not stand against a man for any sin or any transgression" (*Devarim* 19:15). 36
11. "Do not follow the multitude to sin" (*Shemos* 23:2). 36
12. "Do not be like Korach and his followers" (*Bemidbar* 17:5). 37
13. "Do not your distress your kinsman" (*Vayikra* 25:17). 37
14. "Do not bear a sin because of him" (*Vayikra* 19:17). 38
15. "Do not afflict a widow or orphan" (*Shemos* 22:21). 38
16. "Do not bring guilt (תחניפו) upon the land" (*Bemidbar* 35:33). 39
17. "Do not curse the deaf" (*Vayikra* 19:14). 39

THE FOURTEEN POSITIVE COMMANDMENTS INVOLVED IN *LASHON HARA*

1. "Remember what Hashem, your God, did to Miriam" (*Devarim* 24:9). 40
2. "Love your neighbor as yourself" (*Vayikra* 19:18). 40

3.	"With righteousness, you shall judge your fellow" (*Vayikra* 19:15).	41
4.	"Support him that he may dwell and live beside you.... Let your brother live with you" (*Vayikra* 25:35–36).	41
5.	"Rebuke your fellow" (*Vayikra* 19:17).	42
6.	"Cling to Him" (*Devarim* 10:20).	42
7.	"Revere My sanctuary" (*Vayikra* 19:30)	43
8.	"Honor the presence of a Sage" (*Vayikra* 19:32)	43
9.	"Sanctify [the Kohen]" (*Vayikra* 21:8).	44
10.	"Honor your father and mother" (*Shemos* 20:12).	44
11.	"Fear Hashem, your God" (*Devarim* 10:20).	45
12.	Torah study	46
13.	"Distance yourself from falsehood" (*Shemos* 23:7).	46
14.	"Walk in His ways" (*Devarim* 28:9).	46

THE CURSES INVOLVED IN *LASHON HARA*

1.	"Cursed is he who strikes his fellow in secret" (*Devarim* 27:24).	47
2.	"Cursed is he who misleads a blind man" (*Devarim* 27:18).	47
3.	"Cursed is he who does not uphold the words of the Torah" (*Devarim* 27:26).	47
4.	"Cursed is he who scorns his father and/or mother" (*Devarim* 27:16).	47

THE LAWS OF *LASHON HARA*

❖ **Klal 1:** The Prohibition of Speaking *Lashon Hara*, and the Severity of Its Punishment

1.	The definition of *lashon hara*	48
2.	The *aveiros* involved in *lashon hara*	48
3.	The severe punishment for a *baal lashon hara*	49
4.	The punishment for *lashon hara* in this world and the next	49
5.	*Lashon hara* is forbidden even when solicited	50
6.	Refraining from *lashon hara* at the expense of one's livelihood	50

7.	Refraining from *lashon hara* at the expense of one's reputation	51
8.	*Lashon hara* in writing or any other means of communication	51
9.	Including oneself in the *lashon hara*	51

❖ Klal 2: *Lashon Hara* Spoken in the Presence of Three People

1.	Speaking *lashon hara* before one or several people	52
2.	Speaking ambiguous *lashon hara* before three people	52
3.	Repeating *lashon hara* that was spoken before three people	53
4.	Hearsay that the *lashon hara* was spoken before three	53
5.	*Lashon hara* spoken in the presence of *yirei Shamayim* or relatives	54
6.	Repeating *lashon hara* in a different city	54
7–8.	*Lashon hara* spoken with a warning not to repeat it	55
9.	Not embellishing *lashon hara*	56
10.	To whom may it be repeated?	56
11.	City council meetings	57
12.	Mocking a public speaker	58
13.	Business secrets	58

❖ Klal 3: *Lashon Hara* in the Subject's Presence, as a Joke, or without Revealing the Subject's Name

1.	*Lashon hara*	59
2.	*Lashon hara* in the subject's presence	59
3.	*Lashon hara* as a joke	60
4.	Concealing the subject's name; causing indirect damage	60
5.	Underhanded *lashon hara*	61
6.	Harmless *lashon hara*	61
7.	Judging favorably	62
8.	*Lashon hara* against the guilty	62

❖ Klal 4: *Lashon Hara* regarding Faults in Religious Observance

1.	Religious observance	63
2.	Major or minor misdeeds	63
3.	An average person who was caught sinning	64

Index 151

4.	Intentional sins	64
5–6.	When admonishment does not suffice	65
7.	Degrading the wicked	66
8.	A person who does not comply with the ruling of Beis Din	66
9.	Character flaws	67
10.	Warning others not to learn bad traits	67
11.	Inquiring about a person for business or *shidduchim*	68
12.	*Teshuvah* for *lashon hara*	69

❧ Klal 5: *Lashon Hara* regarding Faults in Matters Bein Adam L'Chaveiro

1.	Disgracing a person for his faults in personal interactions	70
2.	Disgracing a person for his inadequacies	71
3.	Disgracing a person for his inadequacies (continued)	72
4.	Disgracing a person for his inadequacy in Torah	72
5.	Disgracing a person for his lack of strength or wealth	73
6.	*Lashon hara* depends upon the subject	73
7.	Degrading a person's possessions	74
8.	Two people who speak *lashon hara*	74

❧ Klal 6: Listening to and Believing *Lashon Hara*

1.	Accepting *lashon hara*	75
2.	Listening to *lashon hara*	75
3.	Avoiding *lashon hara*	76
4.	When is it a mitzvah to listen to *lashon hara*?	76
5.	If one finds himself among gossipers	77
6.	Joining a group of gossipers	77
7.	Listening to an unfavorable judgment	78
8.	A God-fearing person who could be judged favorably	78
9.	Whatever may not be spoken may not be believed	79
10.	Suspecting *lashon hara* to be true	79
11.	Acting upon *lashon hara*	80
12.	*Teshuvah* for accepting *lashon hara*	80

❧ Klal 7: Details of the Laws of Accepting *Lashon Hara*

| 1. | *Lashon hara* spoken before a large audience | 81 |
| 2. | *Lashon hara* spoken in the subject's presence | 81 |

3.	*Lashon hara* heard from several people	82
4.	Rumors	82
5.	Accepting *lashon hara* about a wicked person	83
6.	When the speaker includes himself in his *lashon hara*	83
7–8.	Accepting *lashon hara* from someone as trustworthy as two witnesses	84
9.	Accepting *lashon hara* spoken innocently (*'masiach l'fi tumo'*)	85
10.	Accepting *lashon hara* based on circumstantial evidence	86
11.	Conditions for accepting *lashon hara* on the basis of circumstantial evidence	87
12.	For what ends circumstantial evidence may be employed	87
13.	Circumstantial evidence in Beis Din	88
14.	Not relying on the claimant's word	88

❧ Klal 8: The Subject and Audience of *Lashon Hara*

1.	The speaker	89
2.	The subject	89
3.	*Lashon hara* about a child	90
4.	*Lashon hara* about Torah scholars and ignoramuses	90
5–6.	*Lashon hara* about *apikorsim*	91
7.	*Lashon hara* against the wicked	92
8.	*Lashon hara* against instigators of controversy	93
9.	*Lashon hara* against the deceased	93
10.	Speaking *lashon hara* to one's own relatives	94
11.	Speaking *lashon hara* to the subject's relatives	94
12.	*Lashon hara* spoken to a Gentile	95
13.	Accepting *lashon hara*	96
14.	Accepting *lashon hara* from one's parents	96

❧ Klal 9: *Avak Lashon Hara*

1.	*Avak lashon hara*	97
2.	Praising someone in public	97
3.	More instances of *avak lashon hara*	98
4.	Dissociating from speakers of *lashon hara*	98
5.	Distancing one's children from *lashon hara*	100
6.	Confidential information	100

Index ——————————————————————— 153

❖ **Klal 10:** *Lashon Hara* regarding Matters *Bein Adam L'Chaveiro*
1. Correcting injustice 101
2. Conditions that must be fulfilled 101
3. An additional condition 102
4. Intention to gain practical benefit (the fifth condition) 102
5–6. Publicly disgracing speakers of *lashon hara* 103
7–8. Admonishing the wicked 104
9. Degrading the wicked before a private audience 105
10. *Lashon hara* about matters *bein adam l'Makom* 105
11. Speaking against those who have harmed us 106
12. Speaking against those who have refused us favors 106
13–14. Enlisting help 107
15. Preparing one's complaint 108
16. Defaming one who has defamed us 108
17. Avoiding blame 109

THE LAWS OF *RECHILUS*

❖ **Klal 1:** The Prohibition Against Speaking *Rechilus*
1. Speaking *rechilus* 110
2. The definition of *rechilus* 110
3. *Rechilus* without malicious intent 111
4. Truthful *rechilus* and *rechilus* among enemies 112
5. *Rechilus* under pressure 112
6. *Rechilus* to prevent financial loss 113
7. *Rechilus* to prevent embarrassment 113
8. Responding to inquiries 114
9. Hinting at *rechilus* 114
10. Underhanded *rechilus* 115
11. *Rechilus* in writing; *rechilus* about merchandise 115

❖ **Klal 2:** Public *Rechilus*
1. Public *rechilus* 116
2. *Avak rechilus* 116
3. *Rechilus* that is public knowledge 117
4. Examples of *rechilus* 117

❦ Klal 3: *Rechilus* in the Subject's Presence or Absence
1. In the subject's presence 118
2. Confronting one's accusers 119
3. Speaking *rechilus* to people other than the victim 119
4. Constructive *rechilus* 119

❦ Klal 4: *Rechilus* Known to the Subject
1. Previously known *rechilus* 120
2. Repeating *rechilus* 120
3. Atoning for *rechilus* 120

❦ Klal 5: Listening to and Accepting *Rechilus*
1. Accepting *rechilus* 121
2. Listening to *rechilus* 121
3. Investigating threats 122
4. Suspecting *rechilus* to be true 122
5. Investigating what was said against us 123
6. Accepting another's negative opinion 124
7. Atonement for accepting *rechilus* 124

❦ Klal 6: Additional Rules of *Rechilus*
1. *Rechilus* spoken in public 125
2. *Rechilus* in the subject's presence 125
3. Suspicions and accusations 126
4. *Rechilus* heard from several people 126
5–7. Accepting *rechilus* from a person as trustworthy as two witnesses 127
8. Accepting *rechilus* spoken innocently (*'masiach l'fi tumo'*) 128
9. Accepting *rechilus* based on circumstantial evidence 128
10. Repaying slander with slander 128

❦ Klal 7: The Speaker and the Audience of *Rechilus*
1. The speaker and the subject 129
2. *Rechilus* against Torah scholars and ignoramuses 130
3. Telling *rechilus* to the subject's relatives 131
4. Telling *rechilus* to a Gentile 131
5. Accepting *rechilus* 132

Index 155

❧ Klal 8: *Avak Rechilus*

1. The prohibition against *avak rechilus* 133
2. Praising someone to those who will find fault 133
3. Not mentioning favors done for others 133
4. Offensive *rechilus* 134
5. Keeping secrets 134

❧ Klal 9: When *Rechilus* Is Permitted

1. Preventing a harmful partnership 135
2. Five conditions for the above ruling 135
3–4. Protecting others from harm 136
5–6. After the partnership has been settled 137
7. Revealing damage that was done 138
8. *Rechilus* under pressure 138
9. Telling *rechilus* to people other than the victim 138
10. Warning a purchaser about a dishonest vendor 139
11. After the purchase 140
12. Five conditions for the above ruling 140
13. If the shopper will take unjust measures 141
14. Avoiding blame 142
15. An example of *rechilus* in business dealings 142

❧ *Lashon Hara* in Business

1. Business partnerships, before they are made binding 143
2. Business partnerships, after they are made binding 143
3. Not encouraging a detrimental partnership 144

❧ *Lashon Hara* regarding *Shidduchim*

4. Revealing the faults of a *shidduch* 145
5. Faults that may not be revealed 145
6–7. Faults that may be revealed 146
8. Revealing deceit before the engagement 147
9. Revealing deceit after the engagement 147
10. Revealing illness after the engagement 148
11. Revealing immoral conduct or *apikorsus* after the engagement 148

Dear Reader,

If you have enjoyed this sefer, and felt it to be of benefit for yourselves and others, please consider sponsoring future printings, or our next project for translation, Kitzur Sefer HaChinuch, which describes the 613 mitzvos and their reasons.

HEBREW BOOKS BY THE AUTHOR

ON THE LAWS OF *LASHON HARA* AND *RECHILUS*:

1. *Derech Berurah:* A commentary on *Chafetz Chaim*, and a summary of its laws.

2. *Kitzur Chafetz Chaim:* (the Hebrew edition of *The Concise Chafetz Chaim*), divided into a "page-a-day" learning schedule.

3. *The Abridged Chafetz Chaim:* A quick monthly study and review of the most pertinent laws. Printed in a colorful *"bencher"* format, together with *Birkas HaMazon*, *Sheva Berachos*, and the Ramban's Letter. Recommended for distributing at weddings, bar-mitzvos, and other joyous events. (Also available in English.)

ON THE *MISHNAH BERURAH*:

4. *Derech Berurah:* A commentary on the *Mishnah Berurah*, and a summary of its laws. To date, two volumes have been printed, corresponding to the first volume of the *Mishnah Berurah*.

5. *The Concise Laws of Shabbos:* A synopsis of the *Mishnah Berurah*, chs. 285–300. Printed together with *Birkas HaMazon*.

ON *PIRKEI AVOS*:

6. *Mishnah Avos:* A five volume set, featuring a collection of commentaries discussing proper ethical behavior and foundations of our faith. Culled from almost a hundred different sources, including *Rishonim*, *Acharonim*, the fathers of *Mussar* and *Chassidus*, and other rare works.

7. *Mishnayos Beruros on Pirkei Avos:* The text of *Pirkei Avos* in large, clear print, with the commentaries of the *Bartenura* and *Ikar Tosefos Yom Tov* with vowels. Includes an extended commentary based on more than ten *Rishonim*.

ON MISHNAYOS:

8. *Mishnayos Beruros:* The text of the Mishnah in large, clear print, and the commentaries of the *Bartenura* and *Ikar Tosefos Yom Tov* with vowels. Includes further explanation and a summary of each mishnah, in a clear and easy language. Also includes tables and questions for review, with references for the answers. To date, volumes on *Rosh Hashanah*, *Megillah*, *Beitzah* and *Sukkah* have been printed.

ON THE 613 MITZVOS:

9. *Kitzur Sefer HaChinuch:* A summary of *Sefer HaChinuch*, on the 613 mitzvos, in clear and easy language, geared to help the reader achieve an understanding of the mitzvos and their reasons. (Awaiting English translation pending sponsorship.)

ON THE TALMUD:

10. *Bikurei Asher:* on *Maseches Ta'anis* and the second chapter of *Maseches Sanhedrin*. Includes commentary, explanations and short insights, arranged according to the pages of the *masechta*, as well as commentary on the *aggadata* sections of the Gemara, and *Kuntrus HaChaim:* a collection of insights about the importance of Torah study.

These Hebrew works are available through Feldheim Publications.